Supernatural
Events

Supernatural Events

in the Life of an Ordinary Man

By Jim and Charlene Ammerman

Supernatural Events
Copyright © 1996 by Jim Ammerman
Second printing 1997

Cover by **DENHAM**DESIGN, Everett, WA

Copying for Christ permitted.
Copying for profit prohibited.

Printed in the United States of America.

ISBN 1-883893-48-8

CONTENTS

DEDICATION

To My Wife, who with her gentle but strong spirit, has kept me from the world and on a straight course for the Lord. She has supported me in each and everything I came to know as "the Will of God." She has been a "Biblical helpmate," laboring with me through sunshine and storm: experiencing along-side me the vicissitudes of life and being all that a wife should be and more. For this, and much, much more, I love the idea of our growing old together. Thanks Charlene, for being mine!

Jim and Charlene Ammerman celebrating their fifty years of marriage. Most of the things in this book were shared experiences.

Four generations serving the Lord.

INTRODUCTION

Currently, Jim Ammerman, US Army Retired, Chaplain (Colonel) is endorser and head of the Chaplaincy of Full Gospel Churches. This organization does for churches and ministers who want to become chaplains, what they cannot do for themselves. That is, he represents to the pentagon, and other agencies employing chaplains as the ecclesiastical, responsible office so there will be no violation of America's Constitution requiring the separation of church and state..

As of 1997, this organization represents some six and one half million independent, Full Gospel church members in some 60,000 churches, mostly in 130 fellowships and association of churches. CFGC has 269 military chaplains and 160 what we call Civilian Chaplains who are in VA hospitals, State and Federal prison, industry, and such type chaplaincy.

Jim, and his wife, Charlene, married for over 52 years, live in Dallas, Texas and come and go as they visit their chaplains around the world. God has blessed them and they hope to always be a blessing to others. May God bless you as you read the pages of this book.

✝ 1 ✝

THE BEGINNING

The most influential man in my life was my maternal grandfather who wanted this grandson to be named James after his own father. My father felt that a compromise would suffice and named me Elmer, after himself, and Harmon, the maternal family name. When about 20 minutes old, Grandfather Harmon said I would be called "Jimmy" and it stuck, though the birth certificate carried the other name. When starting to school I found that my name was not Jimmy but Elmer Harmon Ammerman. The oldest of five sons, with a sister 22 months older, I was blessed in having been born into a Bible believing, praying Christian home in Southern Missouri. While nursing at the breast, my mother sang hymns and prayed so that the first things I would remember would be the things of God.

Although Grandfather Harmon had two sons, six red headed daughters and grandchildren by the dozens, literally, yet, I was somehow a favorite. My name was shortened to 'Jim' when I returned from World War II. I would spend hours each week learning from my beloved Grandfather. Most of all I learned the Bible and God's thoughts from this family patriarch, from this self made man who had only gone to the third grade in school. Grandpa Harmon never stopped reading and learning until he died at 90 years of age.

Hard times came when the stock market crashed in 1929 and the depression started setting in. With my parents, sister and a new brother, we arrived in Conway Missouri on October 31, 1930 to live with my Grandparents, for a short time.

While there, a call came one day to get up to the towns little bank right away. The trustees had taken the money and burned the bank so there would be no records. I stood between Grandpa and Dad, holding each of their hands. I couldn't fully understand but I knew from the looks on their faces that this was very serious. Federal insurance for banks had not yet come into being.

Because of having suffered a heart attack, Grandpa had sold two good river bottom farms and put the money in the bank. He was to be able to live comfortably for the rest of his life on the two percent interest he was being paid. At the farm sale he had kept one wagon, one plow, one of everything, even a team of horses which he had to rent pasture for when he moved into the little town. Folks thought it was poor judgment to keep them but he so loved farming he just couldn't bring himself to part with all of it. This was the Lord's provision for what was to come. After the stock market crash and the bank failure, he started doing custom plowing for gardens, hauling and other farm odd jobs. In the fall of the year he and Dad went around the country butchering hogs and calves. They were generally paid in meat which helped feed the family.

It was thought in those years if one had heart trouble they should sit down and do nothing. Because of the exercise Granddad was forced to do to eat, he lived to be ninety years old.

Soon Dad had leased a farm and was stocking it with cattle, horses, and other essentials for farming. By March of 1931 things seemed well until tragedy struck again. While the entire family was in town on a Saturday, the farm house burned to the ground. The owner had insurance. At that junction in American history, many insurance policies got "hot". The Ammermans had no insurance. This burnout didn't bother me as it meant moving back in with Grandpa Harmon.

We lived there for several months while Dad cut down the trees, prepared the logs, split the shingles and built a one room log cabin on a friends timbered land. I went with Dad each day, some three miles on foot, to the cabin building location. I carried cool water from the spring, learned to shoot squirrels and rabbits, and fish from the spring branch, all before my sixth birthday.

My folks managed to buy me one pair of overalls at the beginning of each school year. I could wear them for the first day of school but then had to keep them for going to church for the rest of the year. One year on that first day the boys were entertaining themselves at recess by jumping over a barbed wire fence which surrounded the play ground. After they had all cleared one height they would raise it a bit to see who could clear the next height. Of course they couldn't tell how high they could jump until they failed. When it was just past my maximum, I caught my new overalls at the bottom of the leg and ripped them all the way up to the pockets. Mom sewed up the rip and that is what I wore to church for the coming year.

On another occasion a cigarette ash blew my way and I discovered it only when it got hot. Mom again patched it but she only had a piece of material from a very old faded pair to place a nickel sized circle in the middle of the fly of my dark blue overalls. Needlessly to say, this caused much embarrassment and teasing.

One of the years during the draught the only food we were able to grow was onions in the Fall garden. We asked the farmer whose land we lived on, if we could hang them in his barn for storage. At least we could make onion soup. The only problem was, the cows managed to get to them and ate all of the onions.

LEARNING TO COPE

Little children can be cruel. When I was a small boy I could not speak clearly. I spoke with a lisp and stammer until I was 13 years old. That comes up later in the book when God healed me. We use to have family reunions and cousins would make so much fun of me and call me by a name that upset me. Sometimes I would hide in the barn and not even come in to eat. That only made it worse but I needed some temporary relief from the hassling they were giving me. This was a great embarrassment and a heart ache to me. Of all the relatives we had, there was only one I never got to know very well. Remember, mother was one of six red headed daughters and two brothers in the Harmon family. Aunt Millie was usually not at our family reunions. When she was there she usually was by herself. Not much was ever said about Aunt Millie in my presence. I remember when she once was at a family gathering, I asked my parents later why Aunt Millie smelled so funny. She smelled like a bar rag only I didn't know what a bar rag was. When she walked she often staggered and seemed not to see very well. I was simply was told not to talk about it. The fact of the matter was, as I became older I found Aunt Millie was an alcoholic and her husband and son were boot-leggers. One, or both died in the state penitentiary. These were Prohibition Days.

On one occasion Aunt Millie had some broken bones in a car wreck running from the police. With a broken leg she dragged herself to the car and broke all of the Mason jars with 'white lightening' in it so they had no proof. With no evidence they couldn't be accused of a crime. Her husband was unconscious.

You would think I wouldn't remember much about Aunt Millie but she played a very important part in my life. There is some Indian blood in the Ammerman line as my Grandfather Ammerman had been an Indian Scout in the territory of Oklahoma before it was a state and later he had been an Indian Agent and helped run one of the reservations there. Later he met and married his wife in Kentucky, who was full blood Cherokee Indian. In the "Trail of Tears", as it is called in our history when they moved the Cherokees from the Carolinas and Florida to the midwest, some had escaped. My grandmother and her mother had somehow escaped and were working at a farm where she met and married my Grandfather.

Aunt Millie realized how the cousins were teasing me and she realized my pain. Knowing there was Indian blood in the Ammermans, she would call me over to her, put her arm around me and said, "How is my little Indian Chief today"? I leaned up against her and felt real tall. I was needing her support. In spite of her problems, she was sensitive to the feelings of one of many children there.

As time went on, I lost touch with Aunt Millie, went off to World War II and had not seen her from 1940 until 1967. While I was on leave in route to Viet Nam I went to Kansas City to visit my parents. I asked Mother if Aunt Millie was still alive and did she know where she was.

She said, "Oh yes, we write back and forth some but she is alone. Her husband and son are dead." I asked if she could find her if I took her there. The next morning we left Kansas City early for our drive to Southern Missouri. As roads had changed, it took a little time but we found her. The house had burned and Aunt Millie had moved into an old chicken house that she had turned into a two room shack. As we approached Aunt Millie came out to see who it was as it was seldom anyone drove down that lane. Mother got out and Aunt Millie's eyes weren't good but when she got close enough to recognize Mother she was so thrilled to see her sister Lelah. They embraced awhile and then she turned to see who had driven her there. I was standing near the front of the car and as she approached she said, "Well, if it isn't my Big

Indian Chief. I knew she recognized me after all of those years. I embraced her and together we walked down to where she lived.

She said, "I don't have anything to offer you to eat but if Jimmy will take the bucket and go to the spring, we can have a glass of cold water. Of course I did. I don't remember just what all we did but we stayed four or five hours reminiscing old times and people. She may have been what was called the Black Sheep of the family but she had a heart of compassion for someone else when they were hurting because she knew what hurts were.

After we had reestablished acquaintances and bonds between us, and there had been a bond between Aunt Millie and I because she had always been good to me, I said "Aunt Millie, I am an Army Chaplain now, would it be aright if I went to the car and got my Bible and read some from God's word?"

She answered she would like that. She was much older than my mother. After we had gone through scriptures for awhile I said, "Aunt Millie, would it be all right if we prayed together?" She said, "Oh yes, that would be fine Jimmy."

After praying for her I asked her if she would like to ask Jesus to be her Savior and Lord?"

She thought seriously for a moment before stating that yes, she would. I helped her to pray a prayer of salvation. The three of us prayed and rejoiced together in her new found salvation, after all of those years of living a pretty rough life. Finally it came time to go as we had promised my father we would be home in time for dinner.

Mom and I drove away and I thought as we went, I was probably the only person on earth who could have had such an opening into the heart of Aunt Millie and after those years still be able to talk quite freely and openly with her, and to share the scriptures so she could receive them. There was no barrier in us doing that.

I finished my leave and established my family there in Kansas City near both her parents and mine and her brothers who would look after her and the children.

I went to Viet Nam and on coming back I didn't get to see my parents for awhile as I was needed right away for duty at Ft. Hood, Texas. When I did get to see Mom I inquired about Aunt Millie, that I had thought a lot about her. "How is she?" Mom answered, "I guess I didn't think to write you, she is dead and buried."

I thank God the Little Indian Chief still remembered Aunt Millie, and went to see her and her now Big Indian Chief opened her heart to the gospel of the Lord Jesus Christ.

As a boy growing up in south-west Missouri, we all knew each other in a little town of five hundred people. That had it's good and it's bad points. We also visited church with each other. We had a Catholic church but almost no one visited there. It was a very small congregation. The Baptist and Methodist regularly visited each other's services.

My father, who was a tee-totaller as to drinking habits, insisted that I go to the Methodist temperance services once a year. As I finished high school a couple of months before I was sixteen years old, I ran around with boys that were two and a half to three years older than myself. So, when I went to the temperance services, I sat with these boys who usually sat in the back.

What was going on at the platform, and what was being interpreted by the boys on the back row, were two different things. The Methodists would have some little stands with different things to demonstrate what alcohol would do. One I remember the most, one little stand that was up high enough for all of the congregation to see, was a glass of water and a glass of whiskey. They dropped a regular earth worm in a glass of water and the worm continued to wiggle around unhurt. When they dropped a worm in the whiskey, it shriveled up and died. The object of the story, according to the man on the platform was, whiskey will kill you. The interpretation on the back row was, 'if you drink whiskey, you won't have worms.'

This is something like Tom Sawyer growing up in a small town, who had experiences very similar to that.

From time to time in our town, for several winters, we had a Pentecostal group from elsewhere in the state of Missouri that would come for Pentecostal services. It seemed every time they came it would be an extremely cold spell.

They would rent an old unused warehouse building with a dirt floor, tile sides and a tin roof. They would install three large 'Warm Morning' wood burning stoves that stood about five feet high. They would fire these stove until the stove pipe would be red hot, two or three joints above the stove.

They had a test for the men that came into the Baptism of the Holy Spirit. I don't remember them giving a test for the women. But for the men, the test was being able to run and jump over the top of the red hot stove. As I watched this, I concluded I could not be filled with the Holy Spirit.

We had a man there in town that walked with crutches. He would come to the meetings and "get healed,' but he would be back on crutches in two to four weeks, sometimes sooner.

The same boys I sat with at the temperance services would have a pool of money, betting on how many days before he would be seen with his crutches again.

Young people growing up can be very sacrilegious.

In the fall when I started school in a one room building, I learned my name was not Jimmy but Elmer Harmon. A young 18 year old lady who had graduated from high school the year before and attended teachers college during the summer, did a marvelous job of teaching all eight grades that Fall. By Christmas I could read. No one got out of the first grade then without being able to read fairly well. This was my teacher for three years. By the time I was nine years old I had finished fifth grade. I graduated from high school in 1941, two months before my sixteenth birthday. A year later, I joined the Navy on my seventeenth birthday, but not before some dynamic spiritual things had happened.

SPIRITUAL BEGINNINGS

I was saved at nine years old. In September of 1934, I was in church on a Sunday evening and heard a voice behind me say, "Jimmy, when are you going to receive Jesus into your heart." I thought that strange as I looked around and no one was behind me that had spoken with that voice. I also thought it strange as I had been raised in such a Godly home and Godly church and I had prayed in the Name of Jesus since I was able to speak I had always felt comfortable with the Lord in my life and my own thoughts and family devotions as well as church activities. While I was thinking on this, I heard that voice again, "Jimmy, when are you going to invite Jesus into your heart?" I immediately knew it was the voice of the Lord! My response was, "Right now Lord". I made my way to the church altar, I was prayed for, and questioned by the pastor. With my father and grandfather, both deacons of the church, standing by me, I gave that testimony to the body of believers. It was awkward for me as I had a speech impediment, but it was so good to know Jesus personally, that I didn't care if they laughed or not, I wanted to tell them that I knew Jesus, The next day at school I told every boy and girl in my class how good it was to know Jesus. The teacher wanted to know why I was going around talking to everyone so she called me to her desk. I was able to tell her too. I believe it is natural for every Christian to want to share the good news to everyone they know when they have first found the Lord, that they may come to know Christ also.

The summer of 1938 was a desperately dry period for Missouri, as well as Nebraska, Kansas and other states. All the crops had dried up by the end of May and there was very little that could be done on the farm for the entire summer. Trees were cut down to let the cattle eat the leaves to try to keep them alive. I had wanted to read the Bible through so this gave me the opportunity.

As there was no electricity in the cabin for night reading, only a kerosene lamp, I set in a cane bottom chair under a shade tree in the yard, moving around as the sun changed, from day light until dark. I read the Bible through in a 90 day period, stopping once in awhile to get a fresh bucket of cool water from the spring near by.

At the end of the three months school started again. As was the custom in our Baptist church, we had a 15 day revival meeting both Spring and Fall. At the close of the revival, on Sunday night, after we had returned home, I was upstairs alone in the unfinished loft which was only a floor under the shingles. I had a prayer meeting with the Lord which was life changing. There was no concordance in the Ammerman household, but as I had read the entire Bible through in such a short time, I realized that Jesus is called "Savior" a few times and "Lord" many times. An exhaustive concordance tells us He is called "Savior" 32 times and called "Lord" over 600 times. With the realization of the emphasis that is put on Jesus being "Lord" I prayed this prayer. "Jesus, I had asked you to be my Savior but You are to be the Lord. From now on You can run my life.". Two things happened immediately, three actually but I didn't know the third one until breakfast the next morning. First of all, the Lord filled me with His Holy Spirit. I had given permission to be blessed that way, without even knowing it, because no one in our small town of 500 knew about the baptism of the Holy Spirit. Secondly, the Lord kept me up all night and told me I would keep my life pure, was not to smoke or drink alcohol, and to keep myself for the one girl that God had prepared, that I would meet later to be my wife.

I am sometimes asked, especially by young people, "Didn't you miss a lot?" My reply has been the same all these years. "Yes, I missed a lot. I missed a cigarette hacking cough, I missed emphysema, I missed lung cancer, I missed a hang over headache I missed embarrassment of wondering what I had done the night before when I didn't know what was happening. I missed fights I would have gotten in because I was drunk or irritable. I missed the heart break of spoiled relationships by living a riotous life. I also missed having had VD or even worrying about it. I missed wondering if I had a baby somewhere that I didn't know about or a baby to whom I was not married to the Mother. Those are things that I missed. But the devil would tell us that we missed a lot of fun and good things. The truth is the devil's apples are rotten and there is always pay day someday.

I was awake nearly all night with the Lord. He told me that He had a call on my life, but I kept this in my heart without telling anyone for about it for six years. We were so poor I thought I might not be able to even finish high school, much less go to college. Each fall when school started, Dad would tell me I could start and he would try to keep me in school until Christmas. At Christmas he would say "Well, go on and we will see if we can make it until time to plant crops." At crop planting time I would work from the first light of day until just enough time to hurry to school. After school it was straight to the fields until dark. Knowing every day might be my last, I studied doubly hard. I did not want to be a weak ineffective servant of the Lord and to be otherwise I had to have an education.

In the morning after the night's meeting with the Lord, when I climbed down the ladder to breakfast, for the first time in my life I spoke clearly without a lisp or stammer in my voice. Even though I told my family what had happened, and Baptists did not believe in the baptism of the Holy Spirit, not a member of my family ever spoke against me about it because they knew God had done something good that night in their sons life.

The next morning as I went out in the yard, a neighbor was driving down the dirt road in his wagon, pulled by a team of horses. As I was watching him as he passed by, God told me the secrets of this man's life and they were not all good. This was 'a word of knowledge.' To a 13 year old, it was a very a astounding thing and a shock that these things needed to be addressed to this man. I knew somehow that it was from God. I waved at him to stop and went over and told him what God had said about his life. This was most difficult as I had been taught that I was to respect anyone older than myself and to respect all females of any age. It seemed brash for me to address some evil things in the older persons life. When I finished speaking these words the neighbor excitedly whipped the horses and drove away in a run. This gift of the Lord has been evident in my life from that time forth.

Often times during those early years, the Spirit of the Lord was so strong I would go alone to the woods where the brush was too thick under the trees for people to even go hunting. No one was there and the things of God would come so strongly I would speak them out loud in a prophetic mode. Once the Word of the Lord came, "I will use you to teach Amy officers about Me." This was given to a lad in the fall of 1938 and during that time there was not a soldier in that part of the country. In fact, I had never seen a soldier. The only uniform I had ever seen was one sailor, and yet here was the Word of the Lord saying, "I will use you to teach Army officers about me." I went to the library and looked up 'army' but was only confused as I couldn't understand the difference between enlisted men, sergeants and officers.

I waited, expecting something quickly to come to pass. Interestingly enough when it did not, I forgot about it and two years later joined the Navy, not the Army.

So it is with us that if God speaks to us we usually get impatient when nothing happens quickly and we forget it, ignore it, or even go in opposite direction.

In 1941, after I had graduated from high school two months before I was 16 years old. the family moved to Kansas City, Kansas where Dad had gained employment. We had almost starved for eleven years during the depression and drought years of the thirties. I went along with the family. Until this time I had not even lived in a house with running water or electricity. I had wanted to someday go to the county seat and see the big stone building called the court house, the government for that county.

This was the lad whose bed for many years had been a bag of straw on the floor in the loft of the house. On the better crop years they got new straw in the bag.

When I got to Kansas City, I got a job in an alfalfa grinding mill that made it into cattle feed. I was paid 40 cents per hour. A total of $16.00 per week. Social Security was deducted at one cent on the dollar so 16 cents was all that was removed from my pay. This was a fortune compared to someone who had been use to working from daylight till dark for 50 cents. I could and did buy a car, a 1932 Chevy four door. It was dark green with red spoke wheels and two spare wheels with tires side mounted into the back side of the front fenders. What a classic car that was! What a difference for this Southern Missouri boy now coming to town.

On our first Sunday in Kansas City, the family all went to church. and there was a 14 year old blond girl giving a part in the opening exercises in Sunday School. Charlene was her name and she immediately, that day, caught the eye of Jim. They were married four years later.

☦ 2 ☦

THE MILITARY LIFE

By July 1942, World War II was well underway. I had been with Charlene and her brother Tom that Sunday afternoon when the radio news flash announced that Pearl Harbor had been attacked and World War II had started. On my seventeenth birthday, I enlisted in the navy and went off to boot camp at Great Lakes, Illinois. As I left on the train that evening, my father and mother and a little blond girl were standing on the train station of the platform. As I road the train that night I didn't sleep much. I had never ridden a train before and was wondering about what all was ahead of me. I prayed "Lord, keep me through this war which probably will keep me away for five years or more, (we were loosing the war at that point.) Bring me back safe and in one piece and have that blond young lady waiting for me. God heard and answered all of that prayer.

CHARLENE WRITES:

During the time Jim was in the Navy, I made three dates with other boys. The first time I had a bad cold and couldn't go. The second time, I was in bed with the flu. The third time, I was run over by a car. With that, I said, "Lord, I hear you, I hear you!." I never dated another boy.

After completing boot camp and radio school and excelling so I had been promoted three times, I was shipped out to sea on a destroyer, the USS John Erickson, DD # 420. I made six trips across the Atlantic into the Mediterranean into the war that was going on in North Africa and into the invasion of Sicily While returning home one week after the invasion of Sicily, back across the Atlantic to go across yet again another time, on my birthday we were at sea. I had decided I could go to school and become a minister of the gospel. I had written our pastor back home, who was later to marry me to my bride Charlene. I told that pastor God had a call on my life and I was willing to answer that call. Remember the invasion of Sicily had taken place one week before my birthday. We were headed back with a bunch of empty ships in a convoy on the night of my birthday. But I changed my mind. As I was now 18 years old, I could put in for Navy Flight School, become a Navy aviator and have a bright future in the Navy as an officer. I tore that letter up and when they dumped garbage over at dark, the fragments of that letter went over the side also. I then went back to my bunk and went to bed.

About midnight that night I was thrown from my bunk. The ship was staggering in the water and I thought we had been torpedoed. Actually, what had happened, we had gone into a wolf pack of German submarines and with a pre-arranged signal we were all supposed to turn to starboard, (right) to avoid submarines who were ahead and to the left, Port side. One of the other ships had misread the signal and turned to the left instead of to the right and turned into our ship, cutting a gapping hole into the bow, injuring several people but not sinking either ship. As I went forward trying to get to my battle station, as you go forward and up to the right side , the starboard side, and you go to the rear and aft, down, on the Port side which is the left side. The right side had been struck, the deck was in waves I was hurrying along when I thought I had better feel the deck in the darkness. I stopped and the deck was in such condition, had I gone a step further I would have fallen over the side. I saw phosphorus in the water, glowing from the momentum of the ship that struck us, just a few feet away from me to the right. I couldn't imagine what happened but there God had a meeting with me. He reminded me I had broken a promise I had made to Him. I never went to my battle station that night. One reason you always go to battle stations is for a head count to be taken to see if anyone is missing. I was reported missing, which is a court martial offense if you are not missing and are not at your battle station. After being alone there in the dark and God dealing with me, I heard the 'all clear' signal so I went back to my bunk. My bunk mate told me I was reported missing and asked where I was during this incident? I didn't answer but climbed into my bed thinking that 'tomorrow morning I'm going to be in deep trouble.' The fact was, it was never mentioned to me at all and I never got in any trouble. God knows how to get your attention and God knows how to do good things for you whether you like them or not and God knows how to keep you out of trouble.

While in the navy, I remember having compassion for the enemy. As we took a task force to North Africa, we sank some submarines in route. These German submarines were traveling in what we called 'wolf packs'. They would usually try to hit a tanker carrying petroleum products in the middle of the convoy at night. This would light up the entire area. All of the ships out from that in the task force would be silhouetted from the light of the fire. Then they could pick off several ships before we could sink them.

One submarine had been seriously damaged and I think was running off of it's batteries but it had enough water in it that all of the men in that submarine were dead or knew they would be dead. They were at a depth that our depth charges would not reach them, and they did not, or would not, surface.

We were left behind in the task group with orders to rejoin the task force when we sank that submarine. We did what was called a figure 8 maneuver. We would turn left and come over the sub, drop charges and the next time turn to the right. We ran figure 8s over that sub for about two hours and could not sink it.

Finally our skipper said, "Well, it is damaged so it cannot ever reenter the war so we will go off and leave it. As we had been at battle stations all night and it was now mid-morning, they had allowed us to go to a modified battle station position so we could have meals brought to us and could get some fresh air. All fresh air is stopped at battle stations lest we would sink and the airways would fill with water.

We got to talking about the men in that submarine. I said to my fellow sailors, "You know, I feel sorry for those guys in that submarine."

They said, "Sorry for them!! They are the enemy. We'll kill the ....rascals. (or worse)"

I'll tell you why I feel sorry for them. They have parents back home. They have sweethearts, wives and families, just like we do. While we may be enemies in World War II they are still people and I have a soft spot in my heart for these men that will never see the light of a new day."

The services came up with a marching song in World War II. Many of them I could not put in this book but one I will refer too. I only remember part of it but I thought 'how sacrilegious.'. It went something like this about heaven. "Only Uncle Sam's great hero's get to go there" I knew that wasn't true. Entrance into heaven is not determined by whether you are a hero of the USA or a hero of any country. Entrance in to heaven is through our Lord Jesus Christ. I would never sing that song, yet, everyone marching was suppose to sing it as a cadence to keep in step.

✝ 3 ✝

TO FLY OR NOT TO FLY?

I have already stated how I departed for the navy and later ended up on a destroyer. Let's begin following my eighteenth birthday, aboard ship, July 20, 1943. As a high school graduate and being eighteen years old, and under certain circumstances, I could apply for the Navy Flight program, under what was called a 'fleet quota', which I did. This took six months time, mainly because we hadn't come into a port that had a flight surgeon who could give me a flight physical required to become an aviator. Finally all things were accomplished and I had my packet together and presented it to my commander who had to sign it for his approval before it could be sent forward and appear before a board for selection for flight training. The commanding officer of our ship, the Captain, called me in and told me he would not sign this recommendation as he did not believe in a quick commission. The flight program took between 20 and 24 months, depending on the weather and other factors that were not controllable by scheduling. I did not think that was too quick of a commission but he had been an instructor at Annapolis and felt like that was the route to become an officer in the navy. He said he would sign an approval for me to go to Annapolis for four years, and then if I wanted to become an aviator I could go to flight school for another two years.

To an 18 year old, six years looks like an eternity. Further more I knew that would mean six years before I could marry that young lady to whom I was planning to send an engagement ring. I said, "No, I'm not interested in Annapolis." He told me to get out of his office. It was night time and I went out on the deck of the ship and stood there in the darkness so frustrated because you see, I was having to bury a dream. I started to tear up that application and let it fly over the side into the darkness and the depths of the sea. But I did not, after I collected my emotions and feelings I went below and took the clothes out of my footlocker I put that packet of hard work, hard earned material in the bottom of my footlocker and placed my clothes back on top of it. There it was buried and never I thought, to rise again.

A month or so later, while we were in port again on the East Coast, this time in Bayonne, New Jersey, at the Navy Destroyer Base, I was paged over the ship's P.A. system. I reported to the ship's Executive Officer, Mr. Baldwin. When I entered his office Mr. Baldwin said, "Do you still have the packet of information for your application to the Navy Flight Training program?"

I said, "Yes Sir, but as you know the skipper won't sign it and it is worthless without the captain's signature." Mr. Baldwin told me to go get the packet.

I said, "But the skipper won't sign it."

He replied, "The Old Man is on leave now and that makes me the Skipper. I will sign it as the Skipper and send it to Washington."

I said, "Mr. Baldwin, you know that anything that you sign that has gone forward, you have to keep a copy". Being a radio man I understood procedures administratively. I had been in and out of the skippers office and XO's offices, I had also been on the ship's bridge. I understood the function of command. "When the captain gets back he will see what you have done and both of us will be in trouble."

He said, "You let me worry about that. **Get Your Packet!**"

I said, "Mr. Baldwin, why are you doing this for me?"

He said, "Sailor, I want to go to flight training too and the Old Man won't sign mine. I can't help myself but I can help you. Now, get your packet."

I hastened to the part of the ship where I bunked, got my packet out of my locker where I had buried it and hurried forward to the office. He signed it and dispatched it that day to Washington DC.

Sure enough, we went out to sea and the second night out I was paged to report to the skippers office. When I got there Mr. Baldwin was standing at attention beside the Skipper's desk. I stood at attention by his side and we were both chewed out royally. The Captain concluded by saying, "I would send a tracer after it, telling that I didn't sign it and it is not to be approved but you won't ever hear from it anyway, so I will let it go. Now, both of you, get out of my sight."

We went outside and I apologized to Mr. Baldwin, but he just laughed. He was a very fine man who had been a football player for the University of Michigan. He looked at me and said "Sticks and stones may break my bones, but words will never faze me", and walked away laughing. I stood there thinking, "Well, maybe the captain is right. Maybe I will never hear from them, but still it has gone forward to Washington."

As we returned from that trip to Gibraltar and back, and were still about two days out from the coast of the United States, a radio message came in addressed to our ship by ship call letters. I still remember those call letters I copied so many times in those 13 months on that destroyer. It was NIBG. I knew it was listed under 'Action' heading with information to go to the convoy commander so he would know we received the message. I took the message which was in cryptic to the communications officer who ran it through the decoding machine. He looked at me and said "After the skipper has seen this, I will give you what's in this message because it is for you."

He knew that I would probably understand but he didn't have the authority to give me the message. Sure enough it was my orders to go to the flight school and there was nothing the skipper could do about it. Well, almost nothing.

The orders read that when we came into port I would be dispatched from my ship immediately and have leave until a certain date which would have given me 15 days leave. In war time 15 days was an unheard of leave that few people got. We came into port for some major repairs for several days. The skipper assigned me boiler chipping duty. I was to leave the ship when they left port. During 15 months, I had made many friends. The next morning when I was preparing to go to boiler chipping duty, which is the dirtiest duty you can get on a ship as you are chipping inside the boilers which have covered over with calcium deposits. They didn't even give you a mask or goggles in those days. You would have to come out for air occasionally. The Chief Yeoman saw me and said, "Here is your paper to go over and have your teeth checked at the dental lab today."

I said, "But I don't need my teeth checked."

He looked at me and said, "You don't understand, Here are your papers, you officially go to the dental clinic and have your teeth checked. Now I don't want to see you back until tonight."

I realized what he had done. He had taken me off of the boiler detail. Each morning he had me going somewhere else so each day I had the day off and had a pass, called Liberty in the Navy, to go to town. My friends took care of me in spite of what the captain wanted done. Finally came the day I had all my gear together and I departed that ship. I went home on leave for five days instead of 15.

When I checked into flight school I had specific orders to go to a 90 day cram course at Colgate University in Hamilton, New York. While we were signing and processing in I realized there were some of the best athletes of the universities of those days in my class. Most people reading this book will not remember the names of two quarterbacks whom I had seen play. One was Otto Graham, who then played for Northwestern University and who later, after being in the navy and World War II ended, was with the Cleveland Browns for many years. Following that he was football coach at the Coast Guard Academy in Gratin Connecticut. He was a tremendous athlete and here he was signing in for flight school right ahead of me. When I received my room assignment, next to me was a young man, Ashenbrenner, who never played professional ball and wasn't so well known but he had been the quarterback for Marquette University. I had watched him play in Chicago against Northwestern University while I was attending Navy Radio School before I had gone to sea. I thought 'I cannot compete with such outstanding men as these and I almost gave up. I only had a poor country high school education. I wanted so much to succeed.

As we were getting up at five am each morning, we were required to have lights out and bed check at 11:00 PM. I bought a flashlight which I would use in the closet, sitting under my clothes and with the door shut. I would study until I knew I could answer any question that would be asked the next day in class. Because of that diligence, I finished the entire flight program of almost two years in the top five percent of the class.

That turned out to be a mixed blessing too. As we were finishing flight training some two years later and the war had already ended but they were still graduating pilots as many of the pilots who had flown combat were getting out of service. They still had a need for young pilots, I had been selected, along with several others at Pensacola Naval Air Station, and had gone for a period of four weeks in a "guinea pig program." We didn't understand what they were doing with us. They were testing us in pressure chambers for human body responses and reactions for high altitude flight above 40,000 feet. Some people couldn't stand this and no one knew much about it. It is a wonder they didn't rupture blood vessels in our eyes and ears, or worse. Finally it was narrowed down to several of us, all the way from Ensigns to Captains and they showed us a film on "pure jet" planes. No propellers. They told us everyone there had completed this test program and were qualified to begin flying in all jet airplanes. These would be the first two jet squadrons in the US Navy at the close of World War II.

What an opportunity! What an elite group we were to be with! I had a great decision to make. I went back to my quarters alone. My wife was to leave the next day to join me in Pensacola. Her things had already been packed and put on the train. I also knew if I went in that program I had to sign a contract to remain in the Navy three more years. I knew that God had a call on my life and I could get out of the Navy and start college in January 1946 to fulfill that calling of God. I prayed and talked and turned with God through the night. The next morning I went down with the contract papers in hand and said I would not sign. I had enough combat points to request an immediate discharge and I did. That completed a chapter of my life as two days later I was on a train headed for Kansas City to join my bride and two months later was in college to become a preacher in the name of the Lord.

✝ 4 ✝

LEARNING TO REALLY TRUST GOD

In January 1946 my wife, Charlene, and I had started Southwest Baptist Junior College, Bolivar, Missouri, Graduating in 1947, a two year course with an Associate of Arts degree. This was a growing, special time. The registrar regularly, sent me out on preaching assignments on week ends. Out of that grew full time preaching appointments with two churches. We watched God teach us several lessons, the first being, God is our source. Everyone needs to know that God IS our source, and certainly every Christian needs to know this.

On three different occasions when we had no food at all left in our little apartment, nothing to eat, a letter came with no identification on it but a ten dollar bill inside. At that time ten dollars would buy more than a weeks supply of food for us as a couple. God took care of it as it never came unless we were completely without food but neither did it ever fail to come if we were completely without. There is no way any earthly person could have known the situation.

On another occasion they had made me vice president of the Student Minister's Association of the college. One of the older students had put off going to school but had finally moved there with his family to go to college. He had a bad car wreck and his teen aged daughter had a leg almost amputated. I had not even heard of medical insurance at that time. The doctors were successful in reattaching the leg but the medical bills were terribly high. They had no money to pay the doctors and their car was totaled. Liability insurance was not required then and almost no one had it, including the car that struck them. They were completely without funds.

We called a meeting of the preachers. Can you imagine calling on young preachers who were trying to pay their own way in school, many with families, and trying to raise money for medical expenses from them for a bill like that! That is the kind of meeting that was held. Being in charge of that particular part of the association, I presented the problem. I gave a pitch for everyone to give what they could, to give sacrificially. We prayed before passing the hats. Yes, men wore hats then and it was actually hats that we passed. Before the hat got to me I prayed and asked the Lord how much I should give.

The Lord said, "Give all the money you have."

Well, that was pretty hard to receive, we didn't have enough money to have a bank account. The apartment we lived in did not have a lock on the door so I carried all we had in my wallet as there had been money stolen out of our little two room apartment on occasion. I counted my money and I had $19.00 in my pocket.

The Lord said, "You have some change too."

With that I emptied my pockets and had almost $20.00. I was not a cheerful giver. We had a great offering as everyone else gave sacrificially. We didn't know where any more money was coming from for another three weeks. As I walked home the two or three blocks off campus I was thinking. "Now my wife and I can do without food for two or three days, but we had a baby about four months old who was on a bottle due to a fever my wife had. I thought we would probably have enough milk for a day so. I will get up in the morning, skip class and go down to a restaurant on the edge of the campus where they always needed a bus boy and scrub boy and see if I could get a job. I knew from other students they paid at the end of every shift. This would give me some money in a few hours and we could get by.

I came into our apartment where the baby was asleep as well as my wife. I slipped quietly into bed but as I did Charlene said, "Before your class in the morning you have to go to the store for some milk. We have just enough for the morning feeding for the baby. I didn't give much of an answer so she asked if I heard her. I replied that I did. She knew something was wrong by the way I replied so she said, "You have money for it don't you?"

I had to tell her that I didn't. I had given it all away. With that she set right up in bed as any mother would whose baby wasn't going to have milk after one more bottle. We had a little discussion and I mostly listened as I was the one that had given the money all away. Finally I went to sleep wondering what I was going to do. I expected to have to cut classes.

The next morning while I was getting shaved and dressed to go see about a job, hoping there would be an opening, there was a knock on our apartment door. I had seen an older man at school, whom I was not acquainted with, who had brought his family and rented a house with a little acreage so he could bring his cow for the family to have their own milk. When I opened the door, there he stood, with a glass bottle of milk in each hand. He said, "The Lord told me to bring you this."

As I reached out to take it, hardly able to contain my feelings, he handed me also a $20.00 bill He said, "Here, the Lord said to bring you this also."

Before I could collect my wits and emotions to thank him for it, he turned around and left. I learned a great lesson. I had done what God said to do and before the baby even got hungry there was milk and the money that had been given away. We truly learned that God will take care of you.

I finished the two years work for the school in one and a half years by going one summer. As Spring came in 1947, I had preached at a church east of the college there in Southern Missouri in a little town of Grove Springs. They wanted us to return so we did. They then asked us to come as pastor but we felt we should finish school as it was only a Junior college we were completing. They insisted so much we wondered if we were the ones missing God. We were working hard in school, carrying more than a full load. We were worn out from the trip over on Saturday as our old car had to be driven slowly. We were spending the night in a couple's home with whom we are still close friends after all of these years. We told the Lord we were too tired to stay up seeking the answer. If He wanted us there as pastor, just wake us up at midnight. We then fell into bed and were soon fast asleep. The next thing we knew we each were awake and realized the other one was also stirring. We looked at the clock, and — you guessed it. It was exactly midnight.

We went to that church when graduation was over a month later and stayed there for over a year. God did many things and the church prospered in every way. It had never been more than two Sundays a month of service. We asked them to try full time preaching and we would live on whatever they could pay us. It has been a full time preaching church every since. We also added Sunday night services and midweek prayer meeting.

One Sunday morning a very interesting thing happened. There had been a big wind storm during Saturday night and broken off a very large tree limb. I went over to pull it around out of the way so it wouldn't block any parking spaces.

As I approached the limb, I realized there was a black car parked behind it. In the car was a man who had stopped for the night. I asked if I could help him and he said, "No, I got tired and just stopped here in the church lot for the night. I told him I was just glad the tree hadn't fallen on him but could he stay for church.

An interesting thing had happened. I had tried all week to work on a sermon and the Lord just had not released one to me that I felt was of Him. I did not have a word to give those people that morning or that night. In fact, I had gone to church early to pray, hoping the Lord would give me some word but it was as though heaven was brass. There was no word coming. I asked him what he did. He replied he was an evangelist. I asked his name and he said, "William Branham". I had never heard of that name. He didn't travel in the same circles we did, this being a Baptist church and him being the man that he was. One of the miracle workers being used of the Lord during the times of great healing services.

When the deacons arrived I took them aside and told them we had a traveling evangelist and what his name was. Would it be all right with them if I had him preach for us. I didn't honestly tell them if he didn't preach there wasn't going to be any as God hadn't given me a message. They agreed so we had him preach and he gave some wonderful scriptures on healing and miracles which I believed in but while the church didn't really practice it neither were they against it. He preached in the morning and went on his way.

A large attendance was there for the evening service. I have never understood why but always on Sunday night in our Baptist churches there was an evangelistic service with an invitation to accept the Lord. I don't know why that was the custom as the unsaved tend to be in the morning services. Only the faithful are there at night. I gave the invitation for people to come who wanted to be saved and from one of the very faithful church couples, the lady stood up and came to the front I knew that Delores Shaddy knew the Lord. I did what I always do when people come to the altar. I took her by the hand and asked, "Why do you come to the altar?" I don't put words in peoples mouths, I let them tell me what is on their heart.

She said, "I came to be prayed for that I may be healed." I said, "What?" We didn't pray for the sick at the altar in Baptist churches and expect them to be healed.

She said, "You know about my heart." At times my wife was caring for her children as she wasn't able to be out of bed. She was regularly under a doctors treatment, seeing a doctor once or more a week and medication daily. Once she had a heart attack in our home and almost died. I knew how grave the situation was and to put it mildly, it was beyond my faith but after all, the pastor ought to pray for his people when they come to the altar. I told her, "Please be seated." I then turned to the song leader to sing another stanza.

Well, down the isle came Mary Scrivener, one of the greatest women of faith in our church. I took her by the hand and repeated my question of, "why do you come?" She said, "I want to be prayed for that I won't go blind. It runs in my family to go blind. My father is almost blind now, (and he was a few months later). I don't want to be blind." At this point I decided the safest thing to do was to request another stanza of the song while I got my thoughts together on what I was going to have to do in a few minutes.

There was a man who had slipped into the back of the church after services had started. I had visited him in his home as he hadn't been seen in public for over twelve years. He had some kind of condition that gave him lumpy, scaly skin that he felt would frighten people and he was too embarrassed to come off of the farm. He would send his wife to town for supplies. He would not even see the rural mail carrier as he didn't want anyone to see him in that condition. I had gone there calling on church members, not knowing the situation and his wife had talked to me through the screen door. Finally he let me in to minister to him.

When Mr. Webb got up from the back and started down the isle, I didn't need to ask him why he came but I did. Sure enough, he wanted to be healed and wouldn't look like that the rest of his life. I had him sit down and the singing stopped. I will admit I had them stand up and tell the church why they came. I then started praying for them in the order in which they came. As I prayed first for Delores, the Spirit of the Lord came over her and something happened which I had never heard of, much less seen. She went down under the power of the Holy Spirit. She fell with her head away from me and I thought, "Oh Lord, she has had a heart attack. My wife was sitting there holding one baby and was very pregnant with our second child. She almost had the baby on the spot. I quickly bent over to her head and started praying. I always was very religious and prayed with my eyes closed but this time I wanted to see what was going on. If she died, I at least wanted to be a witness to what I had done.

It was interesting that when she had the heart attack in our home her husband had beat her on the chest and got her heart started again. This night he didn't come forward at all. He stayed in his seat. There I was, alone with God, with a woman I thought was dying at the church altar. Suddenly, as I prayed, more in desperation than in faith, more frantically than in faith, she started turning over and getting up. She leaped high into the air, hollering, "Praise God, I'm healed. I haven't felt this good since I was fifteen years old". No one was more astounded than the pastor. At that point her husband ran to the front, they embraced and I describe it as kind of a holy dance at the altar (which wasn't authorized in a Baptist church either). Delores is now approaching eighty years old and has never suffered any more heart trouble.

When things calmed down a bit I prayed for Mary but I couldn't tell if anything happened with Mary's eyes. She was about twenty two years old at the time. We visited her when she was sixty five years old. She liked to read and was an artist. She was so excited as she had just been to the doctor and for the first time in her life she had 20/20 vision with glasses on. Remember, her request had been, "Pray for me that I won't go blind." Not heal my eyes. She hadn't gone blind but her eyes had gotten better for over 40 years. I don't understand the ways of God but I do know He is good.

I then prayed for Mr. Webb and within the next few days God changed that condition and he lived a normal life until he died of natural causes in old age.

We knew these healings were of God, and we gave Him the credit for them, but we thought God just chose once in awhile to give us a special blessing. We didn't realize we have the authority to call on Him for these blessings as a normal occurrence.

This was some experience to have in a Baptist church. Needless to say the attendance really increased. People were saved by the dozens and we had baptizing fairly regular in the little river near there. Some of the people in the church didn't like this. There were people bringing their sick to me any day of the week. There were crippled or deformed children who had never been seen out of their farm homes. They would bring them to me personally but I said "no." I felt the ministry we did should be centered in the church. It was of God, not me.

I went to the next level of supervision over the Baptist Churches, called the Area Missionary. I drove some hour and a half to see him. I knew his brother so felt confident that he could give me guidance in what God was so marvelously doing. When I got there and talked to him about it, he asked a few questions and then he said, "Well, I have already had some calls about what you were doing down there."

It hadn't occurred to me this would happen so I asked what they said.

He said, "Well, some are for you and some are against you."

I asked him to, "Please tell me what I am to do."

He puffed on his pipe a bit and then said, "You have baptized more new Christians this year than any church in these three counties so I just want you to go back there and keep doing what you are doing."

With that I got in the car and drove back and thought I hadn't received much help but at least he wasn't against me. We stayed there and the church prospered and did well.

After a year the Lord led me to resign, and go to Springfield to complete my bachelors degree in college. We made plans and preparations to move and by then many people in that part of Missouri knew me. We were given the chance to pastor a church while we finished college. We moved to a suburb of Springfield called Galloway. We had some great times there. God was very good to us even though a calamity happened soon after we arrived.

On the fourth of July week end we had a couple of days free and went to visit friends near where I had grown up. As we were going around a corner the fence rows were grown up with weeds and brush and the corners were blind. I had just said to myself that these corners were dangerous on this dirt road as we couldn't see around them. The road really wasn't two cars wide anyhow. The very next corner we were turning to the right with my right wheels nearly in the ditch and a woman from Oklahoma came around that curve and hit us head on. Our car was hit so hard all four doors were knocked open. Our little girl was in the front seat with her mother holding her and we were thrown against the dash with our knees bruised. I had a bruise on an elbow but otherwise we were all right. In the back was our six month old baby boy in a baby basket setting in the seat. No one had ever thought of car safety seats at that time. He was thrown into the floor and his baby bottles in a little box on the seat were thrown out on the ground and broken.

We recollected ourselves and the car was still drivable. The lady said she was from this part of the country and her uncle lived down the road. Take your car to the dealer and find what it will cost and she would pay for it. We made our way back to Springfield, took the car to the dealership to find how much it would cost and called back to the lady. The uncle said, "Oh, she left for Oklahoma last night."

To say the least, I was greatly disturbed. We didn't have money to fix the car, no insurance and she had gone to another state. There was no way I could get the money to fix the car. She had just run off on us.

I found out later she and her husband owned a big interstate business in Oklahoma and Texas. Nothing was ever paid for that wreck. We didn't realize the extent of what had happened but shortly after that, the baby son, Mark, began to have seizures. Because of them we had to be right with him day and night for over three years. He couldn't be out of our sight as he might strangle and die. Someone had to be able to aid him in a moments notice. We had him to numerous doctors and hospitals but no one really knew what to do. We sought the Lord and prayed over him, trying everything we knew. Finally they decided the tissue around his brain was not growing and was compressing his brain. They wanted to remove a portion of his brain.

By this time I was taking final exams for graduating from college. I carried a heavy load as I had finished two years college work in fifteen months. My wife was in Kansas City, some four hours away. She called me and said, "It's desperate. Our little son just isn't going to make it. You are going to have to come as I just can't decide alone to have a portion of his skull removed in such an operation and besides that we can't afford it."

I had one day with no exam, though I should have been studying for the next one, but I went to Kansas City, met with the doctors and returned to complete my last exam. On the way up there, I was driving the first new car I had ever owned. In the summer 1949 if you really looked you might find where there was a new car available. We had found one and made a down payment on it. I was driving up that highway, driving the new car but all the joy of having a new car, instead of the worn out junkers from before the war, was gone. I was praying for my son and my heart was weeping. I realized I couldn't see well enough to drive on this two lane highway and I pulled off on the shoulder. I sat there beside the road, depressed as I could be, crying before the Lord. I remember my prayer of, "OH God, this is hopeless, the only son I have born on Christmas Eve, you must help me. "I couldn't pray any more and while I was silent with my tears flowing the Lord spoke very gently to me.

He said, "I know, I only had one Son myself born on Christmas Day". What made it more touching to me, our son had been born on Christmas Eve. God's only son had been born on Christmas Day. I realized that God knew and had compassion on me, on us, and on our son. I dried my tears, started the car and drove on to Kansas City and met with the doctors. I told them ,"No, you aren't going to perform that operation which you said might not help and might kill him. We are just going to take him home."

The prognosis at that time at that heavy dark moment of our lives was that he would be a dwarf in a baby basket as long as he lived. Here I was at what should have been a happy moment, finally graduating from college, a new car and yet faced with such a future. Having to adjust our plans for what ever was needed to always be with him, twenty four hours a day, caring for that little dwarf as his father and mother.

Graduation day came and I graduated from college. By that time my wife was not going to college as we had two children. We moved to a church at the outskirts of Saint Louis, Villa Ridge, Missouri. I was teaching school as well and putting all the money I could on doctor bills to take care of the son. I told the church about Mark. Some days he could walk, though maybe not straight. He was behind in his growth and didn't talk well. Everyone knew about him and there was much prayer for him and us for our burden.

One of the finest deacons a preacher could ever have said, "You have tried everything with the best doctors available and you can't find what is wrong. I don't want to insult your efforts, but would you consider taking him to see a chiropractor?" That startled me a bit as I thought if the best doctors available, the University Medical Center, The Barnes Children's center, the Shriner's Hospital, all of these things and there is no hope for this little son, I guess it wouldn't hurt. We took him to a chiropractor who x-rayed him and said he knew what was wrong but he couldn't help him. I thought that didn't help much to know it can't be cured. He has received a heavy blow at some time and the three vertebra at the base of his skull are jammed together and pinching the brain stem causing the seizures. We asked if there was any doctor who could help. He said he knew of two, one in Iowa and one in Kansas City. They are the best around and they may or may not try it. As we had family in Kansas City we were there the following week. This doctor took more x-rays. He said it was very risky; we would have to sign a release not to hold him responsible if it turned out fatal.

We went home and prayed over it, returned the next day and signed the forms. After signing he said he wanted us in the room so we would know exactly what he had done if the first adjustment was fatal. We really didn't want to be in the room but we knew we had to. He placed Mark on the table and gave the first adjustment as a very vigorous pop of his neck and the baby went limp as a wet cloth. He reached down and grabbed his wrist to feel for a pulse. We were holding each other, as well as our breath, wondering if he was dead. The doctor turned and looked up at his nurse and I knew by the look on his face that there was a pulse. It had just knocked him out. I returned home and my wife stayed a few more days for more adjustments until he could return home with her.

When Mark became five years old we had to put him in special education to make up for the years that were lost. He had to have speech therapy and tutors but he did catch up in about the fifth grade.

Today he is forty nine years old and pastor of a church. He is a body builder, a strong young man who weighs almost two hundred pounds. He has his own family and own ministry. Praise God, He led us to the right treatment.

Getting back to the time that was spent at the church in Galloway, Missouri, at the edge of Springfield, God truly moved. In one revival we had seventy plus people saved. One was the Sunday School Superintendent. He was a member of the church and thought he was saved, but realized he was not. The training union director was also saved.

On one occasion I went to visit a farm home that the city had grown around. I noticed there was no indication that a church member had visited there on our 'house to house canvas' as I didn't have a card on it. We had a color coded card system indicating if the people were our church members, Christians, prospects, etc. One Sunday afternoon I decided to visit this house, though there were three thousand people quite close to our church, we were the only church in the vicinity. Due to the bright sun light I could not see through the screen door even though the door was open. A voice spoke and I asked if I could talk to him. I identified myself and he said, "Well preacher, it won't do any good to talk to me." I asked why it wouldn't.

He said, "Well haven't your church people told you about me?"

I told him, "Absolutely not!" and my mind was racing trying to think if I had been told anything about this house or the people in it. He finally let me come in but could hardly believe I did not know who he was or what he had done. He watched me for a reaction when he said, "I'm the man who is out on parole after spending twenty four years in the state Penitentiary for killing my wife and baby."

He looked like any other man, he didn't look any harder or any more broken. As I hadn't reacted, he added, "I beat them to death with a hammer."

I thought that was a pretty gruesome thing but I didn't respond emotionally. I asked him why he told me it wouldn't do any good to talk to him. He said, "I've read the Bible through." and he pointed to a large family type Bible laying on a small table, "I've read every page of that Bible in those twenty four years and I don't find any hope for a man like me."

I said, "That's why the Ethiopian Eunuch said to Philip the evangelist when he asked if he understood what he was reading." He said, "How can I except some man should teach me?" I responded, "May I move my chair over by you and let us look at some scriptures." He agreed to let us do that. In the next hour or so I turned to the scriptures dealing with murder, about King David, and God's forgiveness and mercy and that all indeed had sinned. Yet God has forgiveness. I had him have his Bible in his hands so he could turn and read from his own Bible and read the passages as I was reading from mine. Finally he got up from his chair and knelt down facing it, with his Bible spread out before him. He began to cry and put his face down into the open Bible and tear stained those pages as he suddenly realized that by the grace of God and by the clarity of His word, there was a reason for a servant of God to come knock on his door and ask to come in because there was good news for even a man like him. He completely and whole heartedly gave himself to the Lord Jesus Christ.

We talked for awhile longer. I didn't go on my way even though it was getting close to church time by then. He sat back in his chair and I asked if he would come over to church with me tonight. He thought for awhile and then said, "You know, it would split your church. Many of your church members were in that church when I left here and went to prison. This is a family homestead here. They know who I am. Some would forgive the past but many of them don't speak to me until this day. I would cause you much harm if I came."

I told him, "I would rather have those that were left, that would believe that God had grace enough to save any man at any moment then we could start afresh rebuilding a church, rather than to turn you away."

He said, "But that is not what most of your people believe." I could not dissuade him of his opinion. He never came to my church even though I saw him from time to time. I do believe that God had saved that heart of his, that soul of his, and placed his name in the Book of Life for all eternity. Oh, what an awesome God we serve.

Let us now return in our thinking to our church in the outskirts of St. Louis. That was the most pleasant time. The church was ready, growth was going on and the community was growing there in the late forties. America was prospering and the church had it in their mind to build a new, larger and better church building so we started.

Due to a strike, we had trouble getting the steel that was needed for the superstructure. I found a place where we could buy it but somehow we misread the materials off of the blue print and we ordered twice as much steel as was needed. The strike continued and we sold the overage for enough to pay for all of the order, so we got our steel free. God did things like that again and again.

We decided we would have a contractor work for us and build the building but we would do the purchasing ourselves. It was interesting how God directed us in this undertaking. There was as large funeral home across the city. The owner had started gambling and lost his home, new building and everything. The mortgage company was selling him out and selling all they had taken back. The beautiful new oak furniture with walnut trim, were the same dimensions of pews and had all the furnishings needed for our church that had been in his funeral home. We bought it for ten cents on the dollar. God again and again lead us to bargains such as that.

When we were ready to put the windows in the church, there was a funeral held. After the burial, while we were still in the cemetery, a brother of the deceased lady wanted to speak to me. He was from Pittsburgh Plate Glass Company. He asked if he could take the dimensions for the windows from the basement on up in the new church. He said he was an executive of the company and while they didn't do stained glass, they could give us any color we wanted and they gave us free all the glass for the building. When we finished, we just owed a very few thousand dollars that the church was able to pay off in less than a year. God was so very good to us.

We were rejoicing over what had been done, and now would be an easy time to stay there without the tensions of getting the building built and keeping the church body happy. There was a good image and a good name in the community. However, in prayer at home with my wife, the Lord said, "Now it is time for you to go to seminary."

In the natural it was not easy to receive that word. I conferred with my father and father in law in Kansas City. We went to see them and shared what God had spoken but both said, "Well, you have your third child now. There is no way you can go to seminary you cannot afford it financially."

I told them I felt God did want us to go to Ft. Worth. I knew there was little possibility of our pastoring a church while I went to seminary as this seminary is the largest student body of any seminary in the world. There are some men went there for three years and didn't get to even preach a sermon for someone else to gain experience.

They asked, "How are you going to live? How are you going to feed a wife and three children in seminary?"

"I don't know, but God has always fed our family before they went hungry. God has supplied our needs and God has kept my oldest son still alive, walking and learning to talk. He is three and a half years old and I believe God knows what he is doing when he says 'now is the time for you to go to seminary.'"

To save money we borrowed a large trailer from a pastor friend of mine and loaded it with furniture. I went to Ft. Worth to look for a house and employment. I obtained the house and a job as an aircraft sheet metal trainee. We made the second half of the move of furniture to include the family with a five week old baby to Texas in August in a car with no air conditioning.

I started a six week training program which would qualify me for the lowest paying job next to the janitor. However, to complete this training I would have to miss the first two weeks of seminary. This meant if I missed just one day of seminary classes I would loose the semesters credit. The second week in the sheet metal training school the shop Foreman who was in charge of training and the personnel chief came for me and took me back to the office. They said, "You have worked in an aircraft plant before and you have not been honest on your application. Where did you work, and get fired, that you didn't put it on your application?"

I said, "Gentlemen, I filled out the application completely truthful. I indicated where I had been every moment of my life from birth until now and I have not lied. I have never been in an aircraft plant until I came into this one some two weeks ago."

They said, "Oh no, that's not so. You know too much, You know the names of tools, you read blue prints, you are knowledgeable of the different parts of the fuselage and interior of the aircraft and we want the truth"

I replied, "Let me explain that. First of all I am somewhat of a shade tree mechanic, I have always worked on my own cars so I know tools. I have built buildings and the basic principal of blue prints is the same so I can read them even though I have never had even a course in mechanical drawing. What you don't understand, I flew for the Navy as a pilot for two years and they wouldn't let me even get in an airplane until I knew something about an aircraft. The more I flew the more I learned about aircraft. Yes, I do know something about aircraft."

They said, "Why didn't you put that on your application?"

My reply, "The only place you have room for on the application for military service only has one line for the answer. I put down - from July 1942 through November 1945 - US Navy - Honorable discharge."

They talked to me awhile and said that they now believed me and would I step outside a few minutes. I waited and they called me back in and asked if I could go to work that very night in the experimental flight test hanger. I was so overwhelmed to know I didn't have to miss class time in seminary. Knowing that I would have a night job, which is what I must have to go to school in the day time I couldn't even answer. They thought I didn't want to work nights. They began to explain that working nights I would not only have more pay at that job in the experimental hanger but that I would draw a night shift differential. Then they said what they would really like for me to do was work on the midnight till morning shift where they prepare the planes for flight. That gets a second differential-plus pay. I was sitting there quiet so they added, "Not only that, you will be there, including lunch time, only seven and one half hours and would draw eight hours pay."

By now I could almost shout "Hallelujah" as time was very important to me, also, I would be in a job that would draw added pay and require less time on the job. I told them I would do that.

They said, "OK, we would like for you to begin tonight at eleven o'clock. Can you be there as you will need a little time to get oriented before the shift begins at midnight to work until seven thirty in the morning. You will also need to buy some personal tools." They then gave me the tool list.

I went home, did some tool shopping, got a little bit of sleep and came back for work. I was already working on that job before school started a couple of weeks later. God, who had told me it is time now to go to Seminary, had taken care of exactly what we needed in a way I would never have thought to ask. He was supplying for us more abundantly in three weeks time than I expected in the three years projected for seminary. He was taking care of me and my family.

I not only worked in the aircraft plant at night but a pastor from Oklahoma had come through St. Louis on his vacation. He saw the new church building we had built. He stopped and asked about the church and said he would like to meet the pastor. They told him I had gone to Ft. Worth for Seminary so he asked for my name. He wanted to call me as they had churches in Oklahoma that needed someone to preach at churches there on Sundays. I ended up preaching in Oklahoma every Sunday for the years I was there to complete graduate studies.

✝ 5 ✝

THE ARMY CHAPLAINCY

I completed seminary, needless to say, with heavy, long term fatigue, but graduated in God's time frame.

In the meantime the Korea war came along and they needed chaplains. The endorser who had just recently taken the job for Baptists, called me. He had been my Navy Chaplain while I was in flight school. He said, "We need Chaplains to go on duty." I told him I would think about it as I wasn't sure I wanted to go back in Service. I told him I would call him back but here is what happened:

He wanted me to go in the Navy as he had been a Navy Chaplain, and I had been in the Navy, but God gave me a spiritual dream one night in which I was dressed in an Army uniform. I had a parachute on along with Army Paratroopers. We got on a very different looking plane. It had twin tale booms instead of a fuselage that went back to the tail. We got in the plane, took off and went into the air. We all jumped out and as I hit the ground I woke up. Being awake I realized God had told me, "I want you to be an Army Paratrooper Chaplain."

The Army, nor any other of the services, cannot accept a chaplain without an endorsement as it would violate the separation of church and state of our constitution. The Endorsement is a denomination's, or faith group's, approvals which is the determining document as to whether or not a clergy person can serve, with pay, for the government. I knew I could not tell the man who had to give me this endorsement about my dream, he wouldn't understand. When we talked on the phone I said, "Brother George, I want to be an Army Chaplain". He tried to dissuade me. He called about once a month for three or four months, finally he said if I wouldn't go in the Navy, he needed Chaplains for the Air Force. They were now a separate service, no longer a part of the Army Air Corps. He said they would only take Chaplains now who had officer training courses and he had hardly any of these. He gave me a pep talk of how well I would get along with the 'fly boys' as I had been one of them. He needed me and asked if I would consider the Air Force.

I still couldn't tell him that in a night dream/vision God had showed me it was to be the Army. It would have been an easier life in the Air Force for me and less time away from my family. I had learned by now to listen to God and to do what God said. I went ahead and applied for the Army and had everything approved except I still didn't have that endorsement out of Southern Baptist Headquarters in Atlanta. When he finally granted me that letter and it got to Washington, they sent me a telegram set of orders as they didn't have time to mail me orders and get me to the school in New York on time.

I went to Chaplains School, leaving my family in Ft. Worth. My wife had to sell our house and prepare to ship our furniture and join me at Ft. Bragg, North Carolina for our first assignment as an Army Paratrooper Chaplain.

At that time the Army Chaplains school was at Ft. Slocum, NY which was located on David's Island in Long Island Sound, between New York City and Long Island.

About two weeks before the ten week course was completed I was called out of class by the Secretary of the School, who was a very fine dedicated Lutheran man and who later became Chief of Army Chaplains. He said, "Come with me to the office." He had a very serious look on his face and asked me to sit down. He said, "I have just received a call that your wife and children have been in a very serious wreck in Oklahoma". We had to decide what I was to do about the school. I couldn't make a decision until I found out more.

At that time there weren't bedside phones in the hospitals. I had a phone taken to her as she was in traction with a broken body. Her left leg and knee had extensive breaks and her pelvis was broken. The children had been thrown out of the car as it had flipped end wise and rolled over several times. She had avoided a head on accident by hitting a sign post which flipped the car and rolled it over the bank. The car was not a year old but was totally demolished. We still have pictures of that pile of throw away automobile.

I asked, "Chaplain, what happens if I leave here and go to the hospital?"

He said, "We will have to keep you here until another school starts. You have already been accepted to go to Ft. Bragg and you will probably loose that assignment and we don't know where you would be assigned. We would just keep you busy here until another class starts."

I said, "Well, my wife will make that decision." I got her on the phone and listened to her. Her parents had already come and picked up the children as they only had cuts and abrasions. The hospital had released them to her parents. She said, "Well, all you can do is sit and talk to me as I am here in traction. I couldn't get out and be with you. They will take care of me here. You finished those two weeks more of school and then come get me."

I hung up and told him what her decision was. From then until he retired as a two star General he always treated me so good. I asked him one day why he had been so good to me. He said, "The way you let your wife make an important decision and you didn't let your career or your personal desires enter into it, you only said, what do you want? I have always respected that relationship." God even used that difficult time as a 'door opener' to a man who was going to end up being my boss on a couple of occasions and always saw that good things happened in my career simply because my wife and I had a communicating good marriage relationship.

God did take care of my wife. He already had plans for her recovery. You see Ft. Bragg is a paratrooper post so they have the best therapists and best orthopedic doctors in the entire army assigned there because there are so many broken bones among paratroopers. We reported to Ft. Bragg with her in a cast from her hips down. The best care available anywhere was hers. At first they said she wouldn't ever walk again but if she did it would be with a limp. But I'll tell you she persevered and she took therapy until three years later she was able to walk with no difficulty what so ever. As time went on she even ice skated and snow skied. God restored our family.

God began that Chaplain ministry exactly as He had in mind. I had gone to Airborne school and I was the Paratrooper Chaplain that God had showed me in a dream. I want to tell you, when I went out to make my first 'jump' and saw the airplane we were to jump out of, it was the same plane I had seen in that dream. I wanted to stop there on the tarmac and have a prayer meeting of thanksgiving but it got even better that day. A couple of hours later, after we had flown around, we jumped out, when I hit the ground, that first jump was so much like the dream I had of jumping, that my first jump was actually my second jump. When I landed there on that sandy soil of North Carolina, I rolled over and grabbed my "chute" so the wind wouldn't catch it and drag me. Then I knelt down and looked up toward heaven and said, "God, I know in ever fiber of my body that I am where you want me to be and I know the devil had better look out."

✝ 6 ✝

OUR GOD IS AN AWESOME GOD

When I was at Ft. Campbell in the '50s we had a doctor's son who was in a bad car wreck and was in the hospital with head injuries. They couldn't put him under anesthetic while they worked on his head and picked glass out of one eye. I stood there holding his hands while they worked on him. I have done this for several people. Their fingernails almost cut holes in my hands from their gripping to endure the pain. I was coming and going, checking on how he was doing, until his mother got there. He and his father weren't on speaking terms. They finally moved him from intensive care told me he was in a private room, third door on the right. This was the wrong door but it was one of those "God-incidents." I went to the third room but it wasn't him. A young man was sitting up in bed with his legs crossed.

I asked this soldier how he was doing and he said "Well, I think I am doing better." They were going to med.-evac me to Walter Reed today but they decided not too. I asked the nature of his illness and he said, "Leukemia." I then noticed black spots on his legs and arms. I asked if he was in pain and he said, "No I'm not hurting at all. I guess I am getting better because they aren't going to med.-evac me."

I wondered about that. I asked his outfit and I knew the Chaplain he had for his unit. He had recently written an article for the post newspaper telling how all faith, the Protestants, The Catholics, the Jews, the Muslims, the Buddhists, are all trying to get to God. It is like they are all climbing up, around a mountain that becomes narrower as it goes up. When they reach the top they all join hands and go to be with God. A lot of people thought that was such a beautiful example but it told me about the true belief of the Chaplain for this young soldiers unit.

I realized what had happened. I had noticed where his ward pajamas were pulled up from his wrists and ankles and there were blotches on his skin. The blood was seeping out of the veins into the flesh. I knew sense the pain had stopped, they didn't move him as he didn't have long to live but they had not told him. I realized this was a 'Godincident" This was God's appointment. They had made a mistake at the desk. My man was in room four, not room three, but God's man was in room three. God's hour was that hour for that young man. I said, "May I sit down and just share some things about God with you. I knew if his chaplain came, he would be given a false hope and he would die without a genuine true hope and salvation.

I asked if he grew up in a church, ever known the Lord, or had he ever read the Bible.

He said, "No, but I have often thought it would be nice to know something about God."

I pulled a chair over and said, "Let's just take time to talk about that." In about forty five minutes I asked him if he understood what God is saying.

He said, "Oh yes, I do, it seems so clear there out of the Bible." After going through repentance and calling on God and we prayed together. I prayed and then he prayed. He then took me by the hand and thanked me and said, "Oh , I am so glad to finally know God and know who Jesus is and to know I am a Christian now." He had a radiant smile on his face.

I told him it was getting close to midnight, I needed to see my own man and go home. I went on down the hall to see the other soldier who was asleep. The next morning after breakfast I went by to see the man with the head injury. On the way I thought I would just stick my head in and say 'hello' to the man with leukemia. The nurses were there cleaning up the room. I asked where they had moved the patient. They said he had died in the night and had already been moved to the morgue. Thank God that He loves enough to send someone at the eleventh hour to tell us about Jesus.

I went on to room four to see my man there, had prayer and he said, "You know, I think I am going to see if I can make up with Dad when I get out of the hospital. Our God is an awesome God.

The 187th Airborne was in Japan after the Korean War and they had a Japanese bear cub as a mascot. They brought it back to Ft. Campbell but it disappeared along in the Fall. They thought someone had stolen it but in the Spring they saw crawling out from under one of the old 'stand-by' barracks one very skinny bear! Now it was almost full grown with the skin hanging loose. It had dug a hole under the barracks and hibernated. As a cub he had a little harness made and, the paratrooper, would take him up in the planes and throw him out to come down with the men. They now made a larger harness and took him up for a jump. The last five men were going to throw him out the door and then jump out after him. By now he had grown up and had a mind of his own. They landed very bruised and scratched on the ground but the bear was still in the plane.

While at Ft. Campbell, I had tried to cultivate the acquaintance of a very fine Sergeant Major who had been selected by General Westmoreland to run the Airborne School which could not supply all of the paratroopers that were needed with two Airborne Divisions, plus additional Airborne units, such as Green Berets. He was the NCO in charge. He was the number three karate expert in the world.

We became friends and many times when young soldiers were fearful of jumping out of the tower or in making their first jump from an airplane, he would call me and ask if I could come to encourage them. On the Thursday when they finished their ground training before they jumped on Monday, I made it a practice to go make the eight mile run with them. They always finished that run coming up a long grade and men who were about to fall out, would fall out on that grade.

I was fifteen to twenty years older than the average person going through that school and I would go there and make the run. If I saw someone having trouble I would run along beside him, take him by the arm and say, "We're going to make it." With an old man, as they saw me still going, they wouldn't quit. The Command Sergeant Major and I became good friends.

For two and a half years, he had avoided me being with him alone where I could talk with him about the Lord. I didn't know he realized what I was wanting but I was pretty sure he was purposely keeping me from having a personal, private conversation with him.

One day when I was there he ask me into his office. He told the Sgt. under him, "Don't let us be bothered while we are in here, don't even let the phone ring." I knew this was the day. We went in his office and sat down and he said, "I know that for two and a half years you have tried to find a time you could talk with me about God. I just want to tell you it is no use, God won't have anything to do with me.

I looked at him and asked, "Why do you say that?"

He said, "You don't know many things about me. I am going to tell you why God won't have anything to do with me. Do you know what my job was at the close of World War II, while I was on General Mac Arthur's staff? As a young man I had fought through the Pacific and ended up in Tokyo. They were having a lot of trials and court marshals, all the way down into the Philippines and other places. There were Americans being executed, Philippines etc. I volunteered for the job as the hangman of the Pacific." I looked at him and realized he was telling the truth.

He said, "Oh, of course I had a cover story of what I was doing as I flew around the Pacific. Most people didn't know who was the hangman."

I asked, "What does that have to do with whether God would have anything to do with you."

He said, "Well you need to know more about it. Do you know what all happens the day and night before the execution?" I had to admit that I did not.

"Well, there is an entourage of people who come by to see the condemned man. He gets his favorite last meal, so a cook comes by. A doctor comes to examine him because if he isn't in good health they won't execute him because he won't be paying a full price. They have to get him back in good health before they will execute him. A lawyer comes by to see if he has any last will and testament that needs to be changed or updated. A representative of the Commander or the Commander himself comes by as a Commander is always responsible for a soldier. A Chaplain comes by many times a condemned man will ask a Chaplain to spend the night in the cell talking with him before he dies."

"In the process of it, he has a cover story, but the hangman comes by. The doctor has already been there so the hangman has his records. He knows that the man is six feet tall, he weighs one hundred and ninety pounds, or whatever it is."

"Being a hangman is a very professional art. He may be a heavy built man with a skinny neck and if he was dropped at a standard chart rate it might pop his head off and that wouldn't be professional. If he has been a wrestler and his neck is almost as big around as his shoulders, you have to drop him a long ways. The drop should break his neck and kill him instantly."

He continued, "I have killed so many people that God wouldn't have anything to do with me. We went through the references about murders in the scriptures and that *all* sin is covered by the blood of Jesus."

He realized that but then, "Well, it gets worse than that. I was in the Philippines to hang an Army Sergeant that had committed murder, I was interviewing him under false pretenses but really looking him over as to his size and build. Through the bars he spit in my face and said, 'I know who you are, you are the hangman that's going to kill me tomorrow.'"z1

I asked, "Sergeant, what did you do then?" He was a very controlled disciplined man and he answered. "I wiped the sputum off my face, turned about face and walked out. But the next morning, he took several minutes to quit kicking." He looked down at the floor.

I said, "Sergeant, that wasn't a professional hanging. That was a grudge hanging. I had already talked to him about if there was a mistake made it was court marshal that had sentenced a guilty man. The hangman was acting on the duties assigned to him in that job. He was carrying out his orders.

I went ahead and looked at more scriptures about God's forgiveness. He then said, "Well, it gets worse than that." At this point I wondered how it could get worse than that. I tried to keep a calm appearance and listen to his story.

He said, "You know, General Mac Arthur had said there were two things that American GIs in Japan, during occupation days, could not do. They could not get married and they could not learn karate.

I had lots of time between my hanging trips and I learned karate clandestinely at night. When they had their National Events, I defeated one hundred and twenty six Japanese in one day. The Emperor had me to his house for a State official dinner. That got into the newspapers. General Mac Arthur had them translated and he read them every day so he would know what was going on in the Japanese society. There was the story of one of his Sergeants being the number three man in karate in the whole world. The top three don't fight. By seniority, as one dies off they move up.

General Mac Arthur really couldn't do anything because the Emperor had entertained me as the guest of honor. I got by with that. The other thing that General Mac Arthur said a soldier wouldn't do was marry a Japanese woman. That held true during the occupation days. I fell in love with a very fine Japanese young lady. I was married in a Buddhist ceremony which wasn't recognized by the US Government or the Army but I loved that lady very much. A year or two later, she gave birth to a little baby boy. I was so proud to have a wife and a son but in the process of the birth, the baby and the mother both died. That night, I was so upset I went out into the darkness of the night and shook my fist at the sky and cursed God. So God won't have anything to do with me."

I said, "I need to read you some more scriptures. Blasphemers like St. Paul have been saved. God's forgiveness is greater than we can understand."

He really thought all of his reasons were true and that God really wouldn't have anything to do with him. After all of his arguments were settled and his understanding of the scriptures became great enough that he could become a believer, we prayed together and he received Jesus as Savior and Lord of his life.

Shortly after that, I took leave from the Army and went to Princeton, a small town nearby to hold a two weeks revival meeting in a church. The day I arrived, with Pastor Sam, he said maybe we should put the meeting off. I asked him why.

He told me it had been discovered that 'The Man of The Year.' "The hero of that town, who was the town treasure, had been keeping double books and had robbed the city out of a million dollars. The whole town is talking about how terrible this is. They are demoralized. I thought it was the very time we should have this meeting.

The First Baptist Church had all of the white collar people and I was speaking in the Second Baptist Church which had the Blue collar people. It was a railroad, mining town. They were strong macho guys who earned their living by their brawn, not principally by their brain. There were a few men in the church but the feeling of most of the ones whose wives and children went to the Second Baptist Church were men who felt like you were a sissy if you went to church. It was all right for the old women and the kids. They didn't want the young ones to go. We had gone on for a week and still no real increase in the number of men.

I called the Sergeant at the jump school and told him I needed him to come over and help me in the revival meeting. He had just been a Christian for a short while and wanted to know what he would be able to do to help. I said, "I just want you to break a two by six board with your fist, and we will get these macho men to come watch it and then I will have them in the service." He said he could do that.

I went down to the city square and got a bunch of the 'spit and whittle club' and went over to the lumber yard and picked out a perfect board so there would be no flaw in it. I cut it twice as long as the Sergeant had told me to. I took it to the church. The 'spit and whittle club' and the people at the lumber yard had advertised it around town.

So many people came we couldn't get inside the church. There was a raised front porch the Sergeant and I stood on. I had the board and a saw. The people filled the yard, the street and the bank up the other side so they could see.

I told them, "He is going to break this board with his fist but first I want to saw it in two so it will be the right length." I sawed it in two and laid the extra one down. So people could see, instead of kneeling down on one knee and holding it with both hands, I had to stand up with one foot against the wall and my knee stuck out. That didn't give me the strength and balance I really needed. He told me to try to hold it study as when he hit it there was going to be a lot of force there.

Everyone got silent as he keyed himself up, whatever a person has to do for that and then he hit. It left the imprint of his knuckles in the board as it spun me around because I was a little bit sideways, but did not break. The inside of my watch just disintegrated. One of his knuckles was bleeding from hitting the wood and it not breaking. I told him he didn't need to hit it again but he said, "No", I'm going to break it." That time the board disintegrated. Splinters flew everywhere. With that the macho men said, "Awe, there was some trick to that. It was a cracked board or something."

I said, "That's why I have the other piece here. Now who wants to come up and break the other one?" There were no 'takers'. "All right, everybody in the church. I don't care if you have to stand up. You have seen this, now you come in. This man is going to tell he is a Christian and we are going to have a church service. We did and thirteen macho coal miners accepted the Lord that night. I gave them a real challenge. I said, "Men, I expect you to live for God. I expect you to clean up your lives. I expect you to be the head of your house, to love and cherish your wife, to raise your children right."

A year later I called that pastor and asked how the church was doing. He said, "Fine, and everyone of those men are now leaders in that church." Thank God for the testimony of the former hangman who thought God couldn't save him.

As of the writing of this book, I am still in touch with that Sergeant, a man who retired from the Army, got a Ph.D. and ran a Christian counseling center for a number of years. He is now in semi retirement but still visits hospitals and tells people who are sick, dead or dying, about the Lord Jesus Christ.

✟ 7 ✟

BAD TOLZ, GERMANY

I received a call from the Chief of Chaplains Office in Washington DC. asking if I would consider volunteering to take Green Beret, Special Forces Training. I was already a paratrooper which is a requirement for the Green Berets. They needed me to go to an assignment in Bad Tolz, Germany with the Tenth Special Forces Group. The family together, crossed the ocean on a military sea transport ship, got on a train at Bremmerhaven and rode to Bad Tolz on our youngest son's birthday. This was a privilege to be assigned to that unit, or any Green Beret unit, a very elite outfit.

The Senior Chaplain in Europe was the same fine Lutheran Chaplain who had me build the retreat center in Korea. I was delighted to have my next Senior Chaplain to be Chaplain John O. Woods who had been so good to me in Korea. Part of my training was to be a ski trooper. He would come down and we would go skiing together.

We were replacing Chaplain Holland Hope and his wife Bernice from Big Spring Texas. They were such outstanding people and had done such a wonderful job of pastoring that my wife was almost afraid for us to be there as she said, "Such outstanding people as Chaplain Hope and his wife. And we are suppose to try to fill those giant Texas size boots of his." God will give us grace and we will do the best we can. I attempted to console her saying, "I will never be a Holland Hope but I can be a faithful Jim Ammerman."

Flint Kaserne in Bad Tolz had been where Hitler's S.S. Officers were trained, and where he had an advance special training for the S.S. Officers. We know what history says about those men. I went over at night and early in the morning, walking around that Kaserne. I prayed, "God, I am claiming this now as Your territory. The devil has done terrible things and had people plot and prepare terrible things, on this very ground and in these very buildings that we are using that were built by the Germans, but I am claiming that You are going to take control of this. The Earth is the Lord's and the fullness there of, and this is a part that which You made. I am claiming a mighty outpouring of Your Holy Spirit and salvation in this place.

It wasn't long, with two services in the morning and one at night that we couldn't get all of the people in the building. I put in paper work which went all the way to Congress for us to double the size of the chapel. When the appropriation came back, we were in between Commanders. The Commander who had signed off on it when I did the paper work and had the Engineering done for the plans had rotated back to America. The new Colonel wasn't in and the Deputy Commander, who was Acting Commander, without telling me, sent the money back and said we weren't going to build a chapel. I found out about it a couple of months later when I was checking to see the status of the appropriation.

I knew people wanting to go to church and didn't have the room. I knew some very fine Christians there. I said, "I'll tell you what. I can't do it but if you will start an American Church down town, I will sign the lease and provide the building for you. When I left, the church was going strong and I didn't think about that lease. Twenty years later I found out my name was still on it. They had a good pastor and were taking part of the stress off of the Kaserne Chapel.

One day the same Commander called me to his office and said, "I hear some of our people started a church down town. That's not a good idea and I want it stopped."

I said, "Oh, Sir, you don't understand. I'm not going to stop that. I am the one that is for it and I have signed the lease for the building." He looked at me and sputtered a little bit and that was the end of that. I saluted and left for my office. We need to do what is right and trust God to take care of us. Many souls came to the Lord because of that church in downtown Bad Tolz that went on for some twenty years.

There was a Sergeant I had met as I had joined the sports parachute club, called The Trojans. I was already a military paratrooper, a Master Blaster as they call them. I had made well over a hundred jumps by then but I had not made any 'free fall' parachute jumps. I went by and visited the sports jump club where they were packing their own parachutes. I realized there was only one or two men out of those fifty or sixty men in that club that went to church. I thought I would enjoy being a sports paratrooper and besides that, I would bond with them around the sports jumping and I would lead some of them to the Lord.

Some of these men had a thousand to three thousand sports parachute jumps. I was a novice. I would talk to the experts, and read the books on it. It wasn't long until they appointed me the safety officer to keep check on it so we wouldn't have needless injuries or loss of life.

Some of the Sergeants were leaving as a team to go to Turkey. They said, "Before we go on this six month tour, we want to be baptized. It was early spring time and the water in the Izar River was melting snow, so cold that if it hadn't been running so swiftly it probably would have turned to ice. We went to the river, wading through a foot or more of snow to get to the rivers bank. I have a movie of this service of the pastor baptizing several in that ice cold water. We had blankets to wrap around them as they came out of the water. They left for that long extended trip to Turkey as born again, baptized Christian. Praise the Lord.

In the meantime, while being assigned in Bad Tolz, a couple of serious, critical accidents had happened in our family. We decided we would take leave and visit England on our first summer there, waiting until we could speak more German to do our traveling in Germany. We loaded our large station wagon, drove to France to catch an 'ocean going' ferry to England. We spent two weeks there and had a great time. It was common to camp out in a camp ground or even in someone's yard where they rented space. We were camping to reduce the cost for the trip for the family of six.

We were visiting friends in an Army Security Agency, in the north of England, almost to Scotland. I was visiting with the Installation Chaplain when someone came running in and said, "Your family needs you quick. Your youngest son has been hurt." We hurried over to the small dispensary where there was just one doctor and one medical assistant.

In Europe they have very high sliding boards on the children's play grounds. Due to the density of people, they have black topped play grounds. There was a long line waiting to go up the ladder to slide down. Our son had stood in line and was ready to slide down and an English maid's daughter who was a feeble minded child but quite large, didn't want to stand in line again so she slid down and then with her strength and size, she climbed back up the sliding board. Our son, who had just turned ten years old, said, "It is my turn. I want to slide." She just grabbed him and threw him over the side, landing on the left side of his head. He was laying there unconscious. Some of the other children were hollering and poking at him to get up. Our oldest daughter who was about five years older, went for help. By the time I got there, my wife had arrived. There in that little medical facility we waited. In a moment the doctor came to the door and asked me to come help hold our son. He had regained partial consciousness and was fighting.

I went in and got him by his biceps. He was a skinny little boy, ten years old, and I was holding him down. The doctor said, "Look." He was sticking a needle in him, starting from his waist down there was no feeling. He didn't even flinch when he was stuck.

About then with me holding him and him struggling against me, with our faces about fifteen inches apart and eyes looking straight into my face, he said, "Turn me loose, I want my daddy." He fell back on the table and his urine ran out. I had seen men die and I knew my son was dying right there before my sight. The doctor said to me, "Will you please go out of the room." I went out in the hall and my wife knew from the look on my face it was desperate. She ran over and buried her face in my chest and we both stood there and wept. I couldn't speak as I was so overcome with emotion and weeping, but I remembered back, ten years before, on the nineteenth of June, 1951 when that little boy was born.

He was our third child. My wife is kind of an independent lady and she said, "I don't want to go in early for the baby to be born. Let's wait until it is nearly time for the baby before we go to the hospital. We drove into town and she had me park across the street and wait. I was counting pains and getting nervous but finally she said, "Take me to the door now. I drove up and let her out and went to park the car. As I came in the door, the nurse was holding our little son who had been born in the hall. That is cutting it too close for comfort for me. The nurse said, "Well, you have a baby boy." Right there in that hall with him being dried off from the waters of birth I said, "Lord this is another child, the second son you have given us. As long as you let us have him, we will try and take care of him but we know that he is really your child."

While there in the dispensary hall in England, that all flashed through my mind and I silently cried out this prayer to heaven. "God, back there when he was fresh born, I really thought you would let us have him longer than this, but if this is as long as we get to have him, then I know that you have taken him back to yourself and it will be all right." I was greatly overcome with emotion.

In a few minutes they came out and said, "We called a brain surgeon and are taking him down to an English hospital. A plane is flying the surgeon in." When we got to the hospital they canceled the brain surgeon, it was too late. They put him in a room. They didn't allow anyone to stay all night so after some hours they made us leave the hospital. We went back to our friends in Harragaate England. We prayed and walked the floor and tried to sleep but we couldn't.

Early the next morning we went to the hospital. When we walked into his room he was sitting up in bed eating breakfast. There wasn't a sign of anything wrong with him, even the mass that had been on the side of his head. We said, "Steve, what happened."

Child like he said, "Well, I woke up hungry and they brought me breakfast."

We said, "No, how about through the night?"

He said, "Oh, the nicest man in white stayed with me all night. Ever time I woke up he was right there. This morning I woke up hungry and they are feeding me breakfast."

We went to the nurses station and asked if we could talk to the man that set by his bed all night. They said no one was with him all night. We said, "Yes, there was a man in white, who was the doctor? "But the answer was that the doctors didn't wear white in that hospital.

"Well, then it must have been a male nurse that stayed up."

"We don't have male nurses. NO one stayed up all night with your son."

It took us several weeks when we would talk about this, we suddenly realized, the Lord had sent His angel to set with our son and he was well by morning. When the first doctor came in he checked him and said he thought he was ready to be released but couldn't understand what had happened, but in the condition he was in when he was brought in, it would take three doctors examining him to sign the release for him to leave the hospital. We waited most of the morning until this was done. They were shaking their heads, not understanding how it could be.

We told them we were planning on going on up into Scotland on vacation the next day and they said it was fine. We should go on but due to the condition he was in when he came in he very possibly would develop a brain tumor. We should take him to a hospital regularly. We did every six months for awhile until the doctors said there was nothing wrong with him. Let him go.

As we talked with him about it as the days went by, he said, "Daddy, I was up in the ceiling watching you hold me while that doctor was sticking a needle in my legs and up on my body. Why were you holding me while he stuck me with that needle." He saw himself laying there on that examining table and saw me leaning over him. He had a near death experience to the point his soul had left his body but God restored his soul and his body. He is forty four years old now and still remembers vividly that experience. Praise God, He is the author, the giver and the sustainer of life.

A few months later back at our duty station at Bad Tolz, I was suppose to take our oldest daughter, Beth to the hospital in Munich to have some warts on her hands removed. There was a schedule only once a month that they would freeze the warts off. We had two other Chaplains there but one of them was on leave and the other failed to come to work that day. We were required to have one chaplain there at all times so I could not leave the area. I was disgusted that I was going to have to call my daughter and tell her she was going to have to wait another month. About then a young MP Corporal who had been on duty had just signed out and was walking by the chapel on his way for breakfast. I said to him, "Bob, could you do something for me? Our daughter needs to go to the Munich hospital." He said he would be glad to take her. In fact, he was interested in her and he was very glad to have the time with her. So I headed about my work and they headed for Munich.

Shortly after lunch, I received a call. The man did not identify himself but I knew his voice. He was the emergency room Sergeant at the hospital in Munich. He simply said this, "Chaplain, I am not suppose to tell you this, but if you want to see your daughter alive, get to the emergency room quick." and he hung up. They were going to notify us through channels that our daughter had been killed in a serious wreck on the autobahn.

I quickly got my wife and we headed for Munich as fast as I could go. When we got there she wasn't in the emergency room. I inquired where she was but they wouldn't tell me. The Army has a procedure for notification. They had been in a bad wreck, her head had gone through the windshield and her throat had been cut. A can of oil in the jump seat behind her in the VW bug had hit her in the head making a gash. One ear was cut half way off. Blood was all over her. Brain waves were flat. They had put her in a room until they could pronounce her dead and take her over to the morgue. They were suppose to from the hospital, notify me through my commander that our daughter was dead. The doctor wouldn't tell me where she was because I had not been notified through channels. The Sergeant had seen me there many times visiting and felt I should not have to wait so when he called me he didn't give his name. He could have been in trouble for it.

A little black nurse whose daddy was a preacher in New Orleans, who had many times helped me make the rounds and pray over the patients, came up to me and said, "As a father, I can't tell where your daughter is, but as a Chaplain, I can take you anywhere in this hospital. Chaplain, come with me." She took me to the elevator and up a floor to a room, opened the door and walked away. There was the mangled body of our fourteen year old daughter. They hadn't even cleaned her up. The morgue would do that. I looked at her and when I walked out of the door, my wife had come running up the stairs and saw which room I had come out of and she ran in there. I walked to the end of the hall and looked out the window overlooking beautiful Perlocker forest. I stood there weeping before the Lord. I didn't have faith to even ask, "Can you restore our daughter?" I just wept. I heard a man come up behind me and I turned around. He said, "Chaplain, I am a neuro surgeon, if there is a man in the continent of Europe that could save your daughter, it would be me but there is nothing I can do. I'm very sorry." Through my tears I nodded and he turned and walked away. I stood there so alone.

I went to the room after a bit. My wife, not knowing what to do, had wet a towel and was just wiping the blood off that lifeless face and hands of our daughter. I finally got her to leave, expecting to have to make provisions to accompany the body home. We received a call that our daughter was alive. We went back to the hospital. She had some memory loss and couldn't see very well for a day or two but she was restored, came back and finished school on time. If she doesn't lift her head where you can see the scar under her chin, and she wears her hair to hide the scar behind her left ear, you can't tell she was ever in a serious accident. God restored even our second child from death. Actually, it was the third one. The youngest from when he was a baby in a basket.

Today, all four of our children are adults, have families of their own and are healthy and well, serving the Lord and we just say, "Praise His name."

One day I received a call that two of our soldiers had been in a very bad wreck. They were returning on the snow and ice from imbibing in Munich They were driving an Oldsmobile and had ran under the bed of a high German truck. It had caught them both in the face and were both in a serious condition.

I went by and picked up the German wife of one of them. I took her to see her husband, whose face was caved in. They had wired the bones to pull his face back out, nose, cheek bones and all, and put a 'halo' around his head. Day after day I took her to the hospital to see her husband.

When he got well enough I witnessed to him about the Lord. Later our Commander said we didn't need soldiers who got in that much trouble so he had him transferred to Darmstadt.

Several Saturdays he drove four or five hours back to Bad Tolz to see me. I would talk with him more about the Lord but he only wanted to argue with me over what I said and read to him from the Bible. I said to my wife, "I wonder why he keeps coming down here when all he wants to do is argue." In the meantime most of his face had healed and the scars were not so bright. Finally he stopped coming and the next year we transferred back to America. That was 1963.

In July, 1971, we were clearing our quarters in Ft. Hood, Texas to go back to Germany, when a car drove up in front of our house and walking toward the door was a young Warrant Officer. A helicopter pilot. As he got closer he said, "Chaplain, I heard you were here and I had to come see you. You don't remember me do you?"

I said, "Yes, but you weren't a Warrant Officer. You were a young soldier near Munich in a bad wreck and were almost killed."

He said, "You do remember me. You thought I didn't listen to you when you talked to me about Jesus. I just got here and I asked if Chaplain Ammerman was at this post. I found out you were leaving so I came straight here. I want to tell you I have been saved. I belong to the Lord now and I wanted to thank you for planting the seeds of the gospel in me so I would come to know the Lord."

I inquired about his wife. She and their little son were in their motel so my wife and I drove into town to see them. We wanted to visit with them and hear the story of how that family all knew the Lord. The little boy was growing up now in a Godly Christian home. When we left to go back and finish clearing, we had the fondness of the memory that good seed sown had born fruit in that man and he was a successful officer now with a wife and son who knew Jesus.

We had a Sergeant who was quite a good mechanic even though that wasn't his assigned duty. It was so good to find mechanics in Germany soon after the war, that if you knew one you stayed close to him. There weren't garages for American cars off post to go to.

This Sergeant had two cars just alike, matching Buick sedans. His wife got suspicious as to where he was spending so much time. She knew where a Gast House was in the little town of Tegrensee near by where some of the Sergeants hung out so she decided to go check on it. Her husband was there drinking beer with a German frauline. The frauline was larger than the wife and she had long hair. There is nothing like an upset wife. Though, she may have been small, she was dynamite when upset. The husband ran out the side door to escape his wife's wrath and she reached in the booth and grabbed the frauline by her long hair and ran towards the door. It was a warm day and the door was open. When they got to the door she stepped aside and threw the German woman head first right down the steps into the street.

She heard her husbands car start. He raced down the winding mountain road towards our camp. She jumped in the other Buick to catch him. There was a bluff on one side and a drop off on the other side. When she got even with him she cut her Buick right into his and they both went into the cliff and tore up the front end of both cars pretty bad. His was worse damaged than hers.

I heard about the incident. They weren't hurt bad, so were at home. I went over to see them to try to put things back together in their marriage but they weren't in a very good mood to talk to anyone so I didn't stay long. He was really upset as both of his cars were torn up, one beyond fixing. I thought I would visit them another time.

A week later they were in the area where he worked on cars and he had found a new bumper to put on his wife's car. He had one bolt in it and this little tiny wife was holding up the other end of the bumper which was quite heavy on that model car, while he was trying to find the hole to put the other bolt through.

I stopped my car and thought I would walk over and visit a bit. She saw me coming and in her embarrassment she got to giggling and dropped the bumper on her husband's stomach. He yelled, "What's going on?" She got to laughing so over this husband, who she was so furious at a week ago, and now she was trying to do mechanic work to help him. It gave me a chance to talk with them. I shared the things of the Lord, though I couldn't tell that it had any effect.

Nearly two years later I was driving down the highway in Fayetteville, North Carolina and a station wagon pulled up and as it started to pass it started honking and motioning me to pull over. I thought something was wrong with my car. She stopped behind me and we both got out. It was the same Sergeants wife. She said, "I didn't know you were here but I am so glad to see you. You know, we finally got our problems worked out and those scriptures you gave us and that witness you gave us helped. We are both saved and we are members of a church here in Fayetteville now and God is very good to us in our marriage and our home."

We stood there beside that busy highway and rejoiced because God cares for people. God cares for the sinners for whom His Son died.

There were three Sergeant Greens in Bad Tolz. They lived as many of the worldly macho, Green Beret men lived. The Green Berets are terrific people. They have to be qualified in at least four military skills plus things such as under water demolition's and other special skills. They are very proud, egotistical people because they are unusual and especially gifted, trained men.

One Sergeant Green's wife always came to church but he never came with her. She was often embarrassed over the things her husband would do. I also know that at home things were troublesome as she would come in sometimes crying, over the lifestyle of her husband. I had decided that somehow I was going to get to talk to him but he didn't want to talk to me.

Shortly before we left in May 1963, I had checked the training schedule and found out the Special Forces team that he was in was going on an all night mountain march. I always kept my rucksack ready and I told the team leader I wanted to go along. The young Captain always appreciated someone to go along for encouragement when it was going to be tough training.

We got into the mountains and a late winter storm hit us. It was a terrible squall. It snowed and the wind was blowing and the chill factor was so great we were afraid we would freeze to death. We got in a hay barn out in the mountain meadow and burrowed down in the hay, listening to the wind whistling.

I had brought a flash light and my Bible along as I was going to try to find the time to talk to Sgt. Green. There in the barn, he had wiggled down into the hay in the far corner of the barn away from the wind's direction. I sat down in the hay facing him and thought, 'I've got this guy cornered now'. With my flash light, there in the middle of that storm, I read the scriptures to him and told him what was wrong with his life. I am afraid I didn't do it very graciously. I gave him a one man tough sermon for he was a tough sergeant.

About the time I thought I had covered all I was suppose to, the wind stopped blowing and we went ahead with the march and ended up back at camp by morning.

I didn't think much more about it as I left in a week or two, and thought I may never see that man again, but at least I tried to give him the truths of God.

Five years later, I was in DaNang, Vietnam. I had been on a two day recognizance flight . When we returned, another Sgt. told me there was a Sgt. Green looking for me. Understanding the Sergeants Green I knew, I wasn't sure how they might be looking for me.

About then the same Sergeant from the snow storm night came around the building. He ran up to me, threw his arms around me and hugged me in front of several Sergeants and a couple of officers. He said, "Oh Chaplain, I have been looking for you since yesterday. I was suppose to rotate back to America yesterday but I heard you were in country, Vietnam. I told them to put someone else on my seat home. I went to your headquarters to see you but you weren't there. They said you were in DaNang. When I got here they said you were over to the Western Border. I just waited as I had to tell you something.

Do you remember that night in the German hay barn in the storm? I am so glad you told me all of that. About two and a half years ago I was here on a tour down in the Delta along the river in South Vietnam. I was the team sergeant but we got ambushed on the reconnaissance mission into enemy territory. One man escaped alive and all the others were killed but me. I was laying there so wounded my blood was running out. The sun came and parched my skin and split my tongue and lips as I was out of water.

I was so weak I couldn't move and I thought surely I was going to die. It rains often, and some would moisten my face and lips a little bit but they were so parched and cracked.

I don't know how many days I was there. I would come to and pass out. Once when I came to I thought, "I'm going to die. What was it that chaplain told me in that snow storm in Germany." I would remember a little bit and I would pass out again. I would come to and remember a bit more. Finally I thought I had remembered enough that I would try praying to God to see if he would hear me. I cried out to God, I called on him to hear me, to save me and to save my life.

The other men were standing there listening to this wonderful testimony but he didn't care. Some were Christians and some weren't Christians, but they knew this man was for real.

He said, "Somehow, I don't think I passed out that time, I had such a peace that I think I went to sleep. I was awakened and heard people coming through the under brush. I thought, 'Oh no, it is the Vietcong and they will kill me,' but then I heard voices that I knew were Americans. I tried to call out but with my tongue split and lips cracked open I could only make an animal type sound. They heard me and came through the brush with their weapons at ready, not knowing what was there, and it was me.

I was med. evaced back to the States. My wounds were healed and I went to church with my wife. We are both Christians now and our home is a blessing, moving in His Spirit. But I am a soldier. I had only been in the Delta about three months when we were ambushed and I thought a soldier like me should pull his full tour of duty so I volunteered to come back. I just finished my year and should have gone home yesterday but when I heard you were here I just had to come see you."

He hugged me again and I said, "Oh, praise the Lord Sergeant Green." He then said, "I will go now and see what plane they will put me on next as my name will be last on the list since I turned down a flight yesterday. He gave a wave and turned around and left to return to Saigon to catch a flight home to his family.

I'll tell you folks, we serve a mighty God. One that hears us when we cry, and especially when we cry out in a great hour of need.

✝ 8 ✝

CHAPLAIN SCHOOL

Now we are, after three years in Germany, with the whole family back together, traveling around the country to see friends and relatives. both in the service and out. I took a long leave before reporting in to Ft. Hamilton, NY for six months advanced course in July through December.

I had arrived at Chaplains School three days early, It wasn't really early as they had told us to be there to do some in-processing. It was the first time they had a permanent change of station, half-year long school for the Chaplains Course. When I got there, I had done everything ahead of time as the letter of instruction had told us to do. they said for me to get all of this done in the next three days. I explained I had already accomplished all of it. I turned everything in and they told me they didn't have anything else for me to do so I could take off and come back in three days.

I took my Bible and went down on the land point where the Hudson River joins the ocean. There is a sandy beach and there was no one on the beach. I took a blanket with me and a jug of water that I would replenish from time to time and I stayed there with God, praying and fasting for three days. I had been wanting an opportunity to do this. I was troubled with what I had seen in America as we traveled on our vacation before reporting in. We had gone through several states and I was troubled over the race riots, the lawlessness, over the fact that sin had come out proudly on main street across our land. I decided I would spend three days on that sandy beach alone, praying.

The sun was going down on the third day. I knew the next day would start a very busy time as classes would begin and it would be a very competitive course. I hated to leave as that had become Holy ground to me. I was looking out across the water, just savoring the final few moments before I had to go back to the Bachelor Officer's Quarters.

Suddenly, there before me in the sky, a number of feet away from me but clearly visible in the sky, I saw a heavenly form as clear as could be. I sat upright and stared at it. It was so beautiful and so real and so majestic. I heard the Words of the Lord come forth from that heavenly form, that said, "The most difficult, trying time of your life is just ahead, but never fear, I will be with you." There was a very pleasant expression on that face which was before me a few more moments and then it was gone.

My career was going good, I was due for another promotion, I was a Major already. I was approved to become a Regular Army Major, which meant my career could go on. I was at the advanced course. I thought, my family is all well, what can be ahead of me?

I also thought, 'I need to share this with some Christian brother and see if he can help me decipher what this warning means.' I knew it was a very real, heavenly warning. There were many Chaplains within three or four miles of where I was sitting and I thought, 'who among them is the most Godly, spiritual man that I know?' I thought of one of the professors there who was a Chaplains that had been stationed in Augsburg, Germany. He was a Bible scholar who lead many people to the Lord. I used to send new Christians to him to be nurtured and discipled. They would grow into maturity and become his Sunday School workers and choir members.

I walked back up the hill to his set of quarters and found he was eating his evening meal with his family when I knocked on the door. I apologized for disturbing his meal but such as astounding thing had just happened that I wanted to share. I would, however, come back later.

He insisted I come on in and said, "I know from the look on your face it is something serious. Tell me what has happened." We set down on the divan together and I related that experience to him.

He thought for awhile and said, "I don't know anymore than you do what that means, but I do know this, God will be with you because He said He would and He wouldn't have gone to the trouble of alerting you if it wasn't going to be a very serious thing. But, God said, never fear.He will be with you. Let's just pray and thank God that He cared enough to tell you ahead of time."

He prayed for me and invited me for dinner but I could not eat at that time even though I had not eaten for three days. I went over to the BOQ and spent most of the night looking at scriptures, wondering, 'what does this mean?' I broke my fast the next morning at breakfast. God knew what He was saying and we will read about that in a few more pages.

As you know, in November of 1963, the president was assassinated. While we were all in class, twenty-six career Chaplains were interrupted by one of the professors, who came in and interrupted the teacher, saying, "I have an important announcement to make." His face was so serious. He later was the Episcopal Bishop for the Armed Forces. We had been friends for years. He was a good musician, he loved the Lord and loved to sing Spirit filled praises. But he stood there with such a seriousness on his face that we all wondered what was this important announcement! He said, "I don't know how to tell you this but out in Dallas, our President has been shot and is in very serious condition."

I had a little radio, not much larger than a pack of cigarettes that I carried in my brief case. I reached down and took it out, putting it up to my ear. About then the announcement came that he had died. I didn't know whether I should say anything or not. Most of us were just praying. Another professor came into the room and signaled that he needed to speak that, "Our President is dead." Military-wide and for our nation, a thirty day period of mourning was announced. When our class finished the course, we were still in mourning over loosing a very popular Commander in Chief.

The completion of the advance course went well. during our time there they sent a personnel man from Washington from the Chief of Chaplains Office who told me they wanted me to go to another assignment with the Green Berets at Fort Bragg, North Carolina. They had my career programmed for me to go to school and other assignments and I was already programmed to go on to the rank of Colonel. I said, "I can't believe that you can program that far ahead."

This man had been in the Personnel business for years, a very devout Catholic civilian who was head of Chaplain Personnel at that time. He said, "We know who the successful chaplains are and we plan for them to make Colonel as they are to be our leaders. That is what is planned for you." I believe I thanked him for telling me, but, said I would believe it when it happened.

The school finished and I joined my family for Christmas. As Washington had told me I was going to two additional schools that Spring and wouldn't be with my family much, my family stayed where they were until school was out as two of our children were in high school by this time. I reported back to Ft. Bragg with the family planning to join me at the end of May. The spring went well, my assignment went well.

✝ 9 ✝

FORT BRAGG, NORTH CAROLINA

We organized a new group, the 3rd Special Forces Group. It's country of assigned mission was Sub-Sahara, Africa. That is why I was being sent to the State Department School, to learn about the culture and history of the nations south of the Sahara in Africa. It was a very interesting, challenging time.

I had one of the finest commanders anyone could ever have. I had the experience of being there to start a new organization. I had always wondered how you start a new Military unit. You have to have paper work, systems, supply and equipment plus soldiers. I got through that experience and learned so much by it, having had such a good commander.

The man who was to be the 1st Sgt. of the Headquarters for the newly organized Headquarters Company was there when we had our first command reveille at the crack of dawn, under the porch roof of the headquarters. There were nineteen officers who were there to organize this new unit that would end up with some fifteen hundred men. I thought, 'this is going to be great.' We called the roll checked our name tags and ID cards to check to see if we were the person whose names were on the list as we didn't know each other on sight.

We had opened the mess hall and we all walked over to have breakfast together. A paratrooper Green Beret First Sergeant came up and asked to have breakfast with me. We went to a table alone with our breakfast trays. I asked if we could pray and he said, "Certainly Chaplain."

After praying over our meal, he said, "You don't know me but I have known you for several years. I was at Ft. Campbell while you were there, in fact I even attended a couple of your funerals for our soldiers. I was in the outfit next door but you had a funeral for one of our soldiers when our chaplain was away. I have some questions I want to ask you."

I told him I would be delighted to answer them. This man was a part of history. He had been in the first paratrooper platoon. He knew things about the army that I couldn't even find in history books. We became close friends as time went on.

He said, "You know, I have never gone to church, I've never gone to chapel, I have never been married but recently I met a widow lady in downtown Fayetteville, North Carolina. She has a little boy, nine years old, and I have fallen in love with them."

I thought that was a good statement, 'I have fallen in love with <u>them,</u> not just her, but her and her son.' What he was saying sounded good. What he said next was even better. "She won't date me unless I go to church at least twice a week with her. It is all new to me. The thing I want to ask about is something her pastor said last Sunday."

It was in the Spring and Lent was coming up, and the pastor had been preaching on "The Person of Jesus." He had told something that normally is addressed specifically at Christmas, how that Jesus Christ, the Son of God, was born of a virgin. The 1st Sgt. said, "Now Chaplain, you know I don't believe that. You and I are men and we know that a virgin can't have a child."

I said "Let's talk about that a minute. First of all do you believe there is a God?"

He stopped eating and said, "Now I may not be a church goer but I am not an atheist. I maybe don't know much about God, but I would be a fool to not believe there is a God."

I said, "You have just agreed with the scripture, First Sergeant. The Bible says 'a man is a fool who says there is no God.' Now, what kind of a God do you believe in?"

He thought a while and then said,"WELL……."

I said, "I know that is a tough question, Please, you just tell me in your own words what you think about the God that you believe in is out there somewhere."

"Well," he said, "He's greater than a man. He's greater than any force we can think of, I believe."

I said, "You are doing all right. Do you think He made the world and the universe?"

He thought a little bit, very carefully, before he answered. "Oh yes, it didn't get here by it's self."

I thought, this man is a good man and we are going to see him saved. Now let me ask you another question. "If God made this whole world, did he make the first man and the first woman? Do you think He did that?"

He said, "Yes I am sure He did."

Then I asked, "If He did all of that and then centuries later, He wanted to have a Son, could He send His Holy Spirit to hover over the Virgin Mary? Could that creative God, by His Spirit, create a sperm in her, and yet she would still be a virgin, right?"

He said "OH, yes, God could do that."

I then said, "Then the question isn't whether a virgin could have a baby or not, the question is, how great is your God?"

He finished eating his breakfast and leaned back and said, "Why sure Chaplain, that would be no problem for God." He stood up to go and said, "Thanks for having breakfast with me. Thanks for letting me know what a great God is out there. I want to get to know that Mighty God."

I felt it would be a blessing for him to be saved in the church in town, so we went our way. Shortly after that he came to me and said he wanted to tell me some good news. "I have been saved and baptized in that church and I am going to marry the widow lady and her son, and I want you to come to the wedding."

Folks, there is good news God has reserved for those who will accept it.

✟ 10 ✟

HEADQUARTERS CHAPLAIN

I didn't get to serve very long in the 3rd Special Forces Group with the very fine commander. One day I was called and told I was being moved to Special Warfare Center Headquarters as the Deputy Center Chaplain.

The Center Chaplain was a very scholarly priest who was often sent off on intelligence missions. He was an expert on Russian and was studying on Oriental Affairs. At that time we were sending advisors to work with the Vietnamese, Fighting had gone on for a quarter of a century in what had previously been called Indo China before World War II ended, and it then became Vietnam. The North and South Vietnamese were divided and a battle was still raging. The Center Chaplain wasn't there much as he was sent on trips to speak at different schools. Therefore, in effect I became Center Chaplain.

One day it was announced they were going to assign the entire 5th Special Forces Group to Vietnam as the war was intensifying and enlarging. President Lyndon Johnson was going to send entire American units over, as advisor units but not for direct combat.

I was called from Washington and asked who I thought should be assigned to go with the 5th Special Forces Group. They wanted to send one Protestant and one Catholic Chaplain. I wanted to talk with these eleven Chaplains under me first, before I made a recommendation. Anyone of several could have gone, including myself but they said I couldn't assign myself, as I had to stay where I was longer.

In the Group was a very outstanding Chaplain who really loved the Lord, Thomas Cooley, who said he would be honored to go. We had a priest who had served with me in Germany, James Murphy. I called him my FBI priest. (Foreign Born Irish). He agreed so I called the Chief of Chaplains and gave him those two names.

The Army had decided the Commander of that Group would not get to take it into combat. That greatly disturbed this particular full Colonel. I want to tell you a bit of the history involved here.

When I became the Deputy Center Chaplain I had gone around to all of the Colonels in command and met them and their top Sergeants as they were the leaders. We need to meet the leaders whether it is in the military or some where else. When I went to see this commander, whose name I shall not mention, I introduced myself as the replacement for the Chaplain who had just left for Okinawa. He had me set down and we visited a bit before he said "Now your predecessor would always tell me what was going on in the Headquarters therefore I looked better and sharper than the other Colonels in command here. I will expect you to do the same thing. Right?"

I stood up and said "Wrong, Sir. I am loyal to the commanding General. When he wants you and the other Senior Commanders to know something, I am sure he will see that you know. I will not spy for you in the Headquarters. If I ever work under you, I will be as loyal to you as this two star General for whom I am working." I walked out. His words came out the door behind me, "You'll be sorry."

He spoke the truth for once with those words 'you'll be sorry'. A few months went by and he was very unhappy because he didn't get to be the commander going to Vietnam. He called back to his home state where he was very much involved in political things, though officers are not suppose to be. He invited his senator to come to the post to pay a visit. That was a very important thing for the General for this Senator was on the Armed Services Committee of both House and Senate. He appointed me as escort officer for the Senator. A Chaplain doesn't have to accept that assignment but I did. While I was escorting him day and night. I was his "aide" for that visit. I was told to keep track of the expense. I kept an expense account but I never was reimbursed.

During the course of this, the Chief of Staff, the man that ran things day by day for the General, was off on a temporary assignment away from the post. Finally we put the Senator on the plane for Washington and I went to my office to catch up on my work.

I received a call from the Generals receptionist that the Chief of Staff wanted to see me. I thought the Chief was back. When I walked in she was typing but she stopped typing and pointed to a piece of paper on the side of her desk without saying a word. I stepped over and read the paper. It had appointed the commander that didn't like me to be the new Chief of Staff, so I was working under him and the G-1 in charge of personnel matters. He was my boss. About then he announced he would see me.

The secretary didn't want me to be shocked when I walked through the door to find out a man who was not the one who was an officer and a gentleman but one who was not my friend. She had done me a favor in tipping me off. She didn't tell me, she just pointed to a paper containing the orders.

Normally I do not salute the man I work for every day unless we are outside but I as I stepped into his office I saluted. He stuck a copy of those orders over to me and said, "read that and you will know who your boss is now." I read them as though they were new to me and said, "What I told you a few months ago goes. I will be as loyal to you and work as hard for you as I ever tried to work for anyone who was in charge of me."

He said, "Get out of my office." I knew it was not going to be a good relationship.

In the military, when a three month period has gone by you can be rated. It is not termed a 'special rating'. Ninety three days later he fired me, had me shipped off of that post and gave me a rating that should have totaled 240 points and I got 50 points. The G-1 had given me his part of the rating and he had given me 120 points. The Chief of Staff, who could have rated me with up to 120 more , called the G-1, showed him what he had written and told the G-1 he would write this same bad report for the G-1 when he departed in a month unless he gave me a bad low report. The G-1 acquiesced and rewrote his report. Together I had 50 points instead of near 240 points. This will kill your career. Plus I was relieved and shipped out in disgrace.

There were four chaplains assigned with me, who were living ungodly lives. Some of them drank with this Chief of Staff. Large military installations often have a one night a month, big poker game. One chaplain was a card playing buddy with the Chief. One was drinking, even when he went in the pulpit. The list went on.

I had been counseling some of them about their life styles. They knew they could not get by with this type of living indefinitely while working for me, and they didn't plan to change their habits. These Chaplains saw their opportunity and they perjured themselves under oath, swearing things that were not true, which contributed to my getting fired.

The Army had me locked up and I was sure my career was over but still I remembered the end of those three days of prayer and fasting up in New York at the end of the Hudson River. I remembered that heavenly appearance, and the words, "the worst times of your life are ahead but do not fear, I will be with you".

When I was locked up, in the dark of the night when I would awaken, the presence of the Lord was so strong that more than once I reached out as I thought He was standing beside me and I could touch Him. God really was with me.

This thing went on for five months before I was released. I was exonerated. The records were changed to show that it never happened. I still have those records today to show that none of those bad things ever happened to me.

I was given another assignment . We took leave and I was to report in to Ft. Derrick. While on leave I was contacted and told the commander at Ft. Deterick had heard I had been in trouble and he would not have me on his post.

Our son, Mark, had been in a Christian Academy in Florida, as he was wanting to be stronger academically. During the time I was locked up, he had a bad case of the mumps. He had been in the dispensary for six weeks. He couldn't walk or eat. He almost died. It was thought he would never have children but God took him through all of that and he now has two daughter.

As we had not told our son, or our daughter Beth, who was in college about what had taken place, we felt we needed to visit each one and tell them personally. We wanted to be with them for assurance and support when they learned what had gone on.

My wife was broken hearted. She said "how can they do this to you when you have worked so hard?" She knew how many nights I was up most of the night ministering to those in the hospitals or jails or sitting up with them when there were troubles in their homes and I was trying to save a marriage. "How, how, how?" I said I didn't know but God is still on the throne and we will continue serving Him.

We went to Florida and found our son had been released from the dispensary the day before. We took him out on the beach to a peaceful setting and tried to answer all his questions about the evil events of my career.

✝ 11 ✝

CLEARING MY NAME

After a day or two we headed back and we were in a remote area in the Florida Everglades. We were running low on gas but we felt we should drive all night as I felt someone needed me back at Ft. Bragg. Charlene said, "NO, I never want to see that Fort again." About then I saw the light of a gas station in the distance ahead. My gas gauge was on the low side of empty.

While they filled my tank I called an Air Force Colonel at Pope Air Force Base at Ft. Bragg. He was a godly Christian man who had been a comfort to my family while I was locked up. I said "Bill, God has told me I need to get in touch with Ft. Bragg."

He said, "You sure do. We have been trying to find you." He named a friend I had been stationed with in Europe who was being court marshaled He thinks if you were there, you could save his career. The court Martial started at eight o'clock the next morning.

I said, "I will drive all night, come to your house to shower and shave. Have a steam iron ready to press my uniform and I will be there when the court martial begins"

I found out when I got there they had tried to court martial him and it had fallen apart so they had appointed a board of three Generals and they were going to administratively throw the Lt. Colonel out of service with nineteen years service. They were accusing him of moral turpitude, of not being an officer of character, wife swapping etc. . I knew it was not true as I had been with him on maneuvers in France. We had time off from training when others had gone to the women in Paris but not this man. I could testify that under oath.

Just as they were ready to convene that board of three Generals, I walked into the room. The Generals looked at each other as they knew who I was. My friend was more than glad to see me. The lawyers said they had new evidence to present. They put me under oath. When I finished testifying the trial attorney knew the case was lost. The Generals exonerated this man and released him back to duty. He got to finish his twenty years in the army. I found out they had promised a two star General that they would throw that Lt. Colonel out of the army. The Generals could have killed me. I hoped I would never have to serve under any of those three.

We continued on our way to see our daughter Beth in college in Missouri, and share with her what had happened to her daddy. Then it was on to Kansas City where we had given Charlene's brothers home as a leave address. While there we received a call to go to Ft. Benjamin Harrison in Indianapolis.

What a beautiful assignment it was. God gave us a terrific two and a half years of ministry there, with three thousand soldiers at a time who had just finished boot camp and were assigned there to become finance clerks, administrative clerks, etc. Some were taking short hand and were there long enough to help in the chapel programs.

The Finance School for officers, as well as the Officers School for the Adjutant General's and The Department of Defense Information School were all located there. We had some of the finest people I ever served with. God did some marvelous things before I left to go to Vietnam.

While we were on leave, in route to Indianapolis, my wife wondered if they would send a bad word ahead of me to the new assignment. I didn't think so as they would want a good job done, but my records still had some bad reports in them. at this time. "When I turn my records in they may question me. I will just give them truthful answers and ask to only be given a chance to be the chaplain that I always try to be." She wondered if they would let me even try. I said "Dear, the promise of the Lord is, 'He will be with us'. I am counting on His promise more than the rest of the world put together and I am not going to worry about it."

We reported there in early April. The problem at Ft Bragg had started on Valentines Day in February, fourteen months before. It had gone on a long time.

Good ministry had started, we were being blessed. It was the 4th of July when we received a call that one of our dear friends was killed in Vietnam. We had been stationed together, he sang in our choir, we had gone on the same ship to Europe. He and his wife sang specials for us. He was a very Godly man. Lee Holt had just been killed in the big battle they had over the fourth of July, 1965. "Will you come to Topeka to have his funeral?"

My commander said there was a special funding code to cover this and it would pay for my going there for the funeral. By this time the commander respected me and he said he knew I would have special friends from the chapels and some others may call. "We have the money to send you anywhere in America you need to go."

I said, I wanted to drive instead of flying as my wife is a very good friend of the widow and maybe she can be comfort to her.

We drove there for the funeral. As I stood over the casket I said "This man is thirty-three years old. He lived for the Lord all of his life, he had as many years on this earth as the Lord Jesus, but now he has gone to be with the Lord Jesus, because this man knew Jesus Christ personally."

We stayed a couple of days and then went to the same brothers home as we had given as the leave address before and spent the night. The next morning we were sleeping in as we were exhausted. My brother in law tapped on our door and said, "Jim, I have a call for you and they say it is important."

I went to the phone and it was my headquarters in Ft. Benjamin Harrison who said, "You have just been put on alert and you need to leave for Vietnam in three days. You need to get back here immediately. You are signed for all the property in three chapels and we need to get all of that released and you to clear."

I told them to get my good sergeant started on taking care of the property and we will be back there as quick as we can get there.

As I turned around my wife was there and heard what had been said. She began to cry. I held her as she could hardly stand up. She said "That is Washington still playing games with you. They want you out of the USA so you cannot clear your good name."

You see, when I got out of lock-up I had gone to the Chief of Chaplains and told him a great injustice had been done to me. He said he didn't believe that.

I said, "Sir, the things those four chaplains swore under oath, I can prove they are wrong in records out of their files, right here in your office. They said things happened at Ft. Campbell when I was in Europe. They said things happened in Europe when I was at Ft. Bragg."

I didn't call him 'Chaplain' then, I called him 'General'. I have never called him Chaplain again until this day. He may have worn two stars but as far as I was concerned he didn't deserve to be called Chaplain. I said "General, I am going to see the Inspector General of the army and file a complaint against you, General, Sir" I did and the Army started an investigation. He had a heart attack and a stroke as a lot of things were wrong in that office. He was not running the Chaplaincy in an upright manner. He began to 'sweat blood' over the investigation.

My wife said, "They are going to ship you to Vietnam so you can't be here to answer any questions while the investigation goes on. This is just a part of the ordeal. It isn't over."

I said "Yes, it's over. I have put up with this long enough." Jim Ammerman is a pretty mild guy but when I see my wife so upset, something bristles inside of me. I'm liable to take your head off if you have caused it. I am just that much still in the flesh.

I had gone to college with a Catholic man who told me there was a Catholic program organized so that they would have people continually in high places. They picked out very sharp young students and had them major in Political Science. Bill Cody had been one of those sharp young men who had gotten a degree in that field. He had been assigned in Washington. Presidents may come and go, Congressmen and Senators may come and go, but these men are in General Service positions and they become very powerful people with tenure in Washington.

I had been in Washington and walking down the street, there was Bill Cody. We greeted each other and I asked what he was doing. He said he was doing exactly what the Catholic Church wanted him to do. He was working in the White House. He inquired as to what I was doing and I told him I was between assignments as I had just been fired as a Chaplain. He asked if it was a fair deal. I told him "No, but let us let the Army take care of that."

He said, "Let me tell you I can walk into that Oval Office at any time. I can speak to the President. Let me give you my card with two numbers on it. Wait, let me give you another number. They are 24 hour a day numbers. I am required to be reachable even if I am on vacation. If you ever need me, call this number and I can help you."

There in my brother in law's home, I decided it was time to call that number of Bill Cody's. A secretary answered and soon had Bill on the line. He asked what he could for me. I explained how they were getting me out of the country so I couldn't be reached for the investigation. He asked where we could be reached. I gave him a couple of additional numbers of our parents.

He said he had the numbers and, "You will hear from the right authorities."

My wife said she would like to go to see her parents in the country where we could be quiet and alone to try to find some peace.

As we drove into the lane to the house, they both came into the yard and motioned us to hurry. There was a Colonel who had called and I was suppose to call him right away.

I went into the house and called. It was a Colonel who was from a higher headquarters above our post at Ft Benjamin Harrison. He said, "Chaplain, will you give me your full name, rank and service number." I did and then he said "You are the right man. I have been told by Washington, to report to the Pentagon in Washington, and they are to report to a special assistant of the President himself, that I have contacted you, and I am not to eat nor sleep until I have told you, those orders for Vietnam are canceled. Will you repeat this back to me?"

I said, "Sir, I want your name, rank, and serial number." After taking it down I said, "Yes, I heard that and I will go back to duty."

He said, "I have already called your headquarters and told them you are not going to Vietnam and will continue on duty there at Ft Benjamin Harrison, do you understand all of this? Now I can call Washington and tell them I have delivered the message, and I can go home for dinner. Chaplain, can you tell me what is going on?

I said Colonel, I am just a Major, but right now, the least you know about this battle, the happier you will be. God bless you, go on home to your family."

He thanked me and I hung up and told my wife, "We aren't going to Vietnam. now. God has taken the connections of years ago and made the system work. I won't go until this whole mess is cleared up."

With a great weight lifted, we had a good evening meal with her parents. We stayed a couple more days and reported back to continue duty at Benjamin Harrison. We had a continual revival for the two and a half years we were there as God was, still indeed, on His throne.

✞ 12 ✞

FORT BEN

When we arrived at Ft Benjamin, we heard there was a lady who was having a Child Evangelism Group in her home. I called her, introduced myself and told her I heard about her class and would she come to my office to discuss it. Ida Lauchner got real quiet and I asked if she was still there. She thought I was going to tell her she couldn't continue the classes. Previous chaplains had tried to close it down and here I was offering to pay the bills. Out of that grew a great relationship. He became our Sunday School Superintendent. We still work together until this day even though he has long sense retired from the service and they live in Richmond, IN. Ron and Ida Lauchner are precious servants of God and we are thankful to know them.

I do not understand people. I don't understand their theology and philosophy that when children's lives are being changed and homes are being reached into with the literature they bring home and someone is against it. I always felt there is more to do at any place I would be assigned than I could get done, or the chaplains under me could do. Why not let all of the laymen and women help us and expand the work?

At the Defense Information School, there were Army, Navy, Air Force, Marines and Coast Guard attending the school. The Secretary of the school was an Army officer that I had met years before when he was Secretary of the Army Chaplains School. He was a very sharp officer who always looked like he was out for 'dress parade'. I was glad to renew his acquaintance. I found out I had inherited his wife as the President of the Protestant Women of the Chapel. Here was a couple who knew a lot about the Army Chaplaincy but in talking with them I realized they did not know the Lord even though they were regular in Chapel attendance, They went on our prayer list. I met with her as she made plans for the Women of the Chapel and she had good plans but it was in the natural with a religious bent.

One day before I had been there too long I was visiting in daily rounds in the hospital. I heard the siren of an ambulance coming in so I went around to the emergency room. To my surprise, on the gurney, being wheeled in, was Mrs. Marguerite Williams.

About that same time the Hospital Commander, who was a very fine Jewish Colonel, Al Throne, told me the doctors said Marguerite was very critical. She could go at any minute.

What had happened was, they had a cabinet door that would pop open and it bumped her on the shin, causing a blood clot which had moved to the entrance to her heart. One little move could dislodge it and she was a dead person.

They put her in an oxygen tent and were trying to thin her blood. In the meantime, it was touch and go. I asked the doctor in charge if I could go in to her. He said, "No one can see her. the slightest excitement will kill that woman."

I turned to Dr. Throne and told him I really wanted to go in and pray with her. He said he had never over ridden a doctor under his command until now. He turned to the doctor and said, "Jim Ammerman goes anywhere in this hospital he wants to and that includes to see your patient."

The doctor really didn't like that but he said, "All right, but for only sixty seconds." As I walked into the room he had a nurse with a stop watch , holding me by the arm. I walked over and touched Marguerite through that oxygen tent and said, "Marguerite, I have sixty seconds to pray with you. First I want to ask you this question. Do you know Jesus Christ well enough, and personally enough to die by?".

She looked up at me and tears ran out the corners of her eyes and down her temples. She shook her head, No"

I told her I was going to pray and God was going to keep her alive. You are going to know Jesus. I prayed for her and as I finished my prayer, the nurse was pulling me out the door as my sixty seconds were up.

When I left the room, Col. Don Williams was in the hall, talking to Col. Throne, the hospital commander. Col. Williams wanted to go in to see his wife, feeling if anyone should see her, he should, but Col. Throne told him, 'no', it was too critical. But I had already covenanted with God for her life until she had eternal life. She did not die but is still alive today. As her condition improved I went back when I didn't have to hurry. Out of that experience she came to personally know the Lord. When she got out of the hospital she came to see me and said "We have to pray for my husband. He is a good man but he is as lost as he can be." He was a good man but it is one thing to be good and another to be God's man or woman. We began to pray. There was a group of Spirit filled ladies there who were real prayer warriors so we had them praying. Marguerite got filled with the Spirit and then she had a new dimension to her praying and walking with the Lord. She had me make an appointment with her husband to talk to him about his condition. I made an appointment to see him in his office and he canceled it, Another, for him to come to my office, and he canceled it.

Finally I went to him and said, "Don, I know you are not anxious to meet with me alone but I want you to give me an appointment. Just tell me when it is and I will put it on my calendar. I don't care if I have an appointment with the General, I will cancel it and see you. It is that important. He gave me an evening for later in the week. I told him I would be there unless I was a dead man and I have your word as a gentleman that you will be at your home when I get there.

I went at the appointed time. I had called his wife and asked for something to visit about when I got there as he was going to be nervous when I arrived. I wanted something to discuss to get him relaxed. She had told me he was proud of a Bar-B-Que pit he had built. When I arrived he was so nervous he was white in the face and had sweat on his forehead. I knew it was God's hour as many people were praying for him at that time.

I told him I understood he had built a Bar-B-Que pit and I wanted to see it. He was glad to show me and he relaxed a bit before we sat in the living room to talk. Marguerite was in the other room praying as only a Godly wife could pray. He told me he would give me one hour. At the end of the hour he said, "No, I'm just not going to do it now." and I knew that was his answer. Marguerite came in with a beautiful chocolate cake she had baked, biting her lip to keep from crying over the answer he had given.

The atmosphere was so tense I told them a story to break the silence. It was about a preacher I knew who had a gift of leading couples to the Lord. He was baptizing a large group as they did each month and the first one to be baptized was a small little wife and she said, "Pastor, my husband is also being baptized, could you baptize the two of us together?" He had never done that, but agreed to it. The husband was a small man so he told them to stand together, both take hold of his arm and he would lean them back together for immersion. They were so happy over it. The baptismal service proceeded well until they came to the last lady who was larger than the pastor and she said, "Oh, I saw that first baptizing and it was so wonderful. My husband is waiting to be baptized also in the men's wing. Could you baptize us together?"

It was almost impossible to say "no "so he agreed. Her husband came out and he was still larger. The pastor tried it the same way he had with the smaller couple. He said all three were under the water and he wasn't sure any of them were going to survive as they were so large they just pulled him under too. We laughed, ate our cake and I excused myself and went home.

Shortly after that he received orders as Secretary of the Defense Information School to go on a visit to Monetary, near San Francisco. He had always wanted to go through the Southwest to see the country so he had the orders cut to go by Greyhound bus. If you can imagine a very tall man, about six feet four inches, electing to ride by bus all the way from Indianapolis to San Franciso when he could have flown in three or four hours. He departed on the bus.

Ladies, you understand what a praying Godly wife can do. She had the people praying and she had also fixed his suit case. When he got out clean socks, there was a scripture reference with a "I love you Dear", note in them. There was a Bible in his suit case he didn't know about. When he got on the bus in Indianapolis he sat by a man who talked to him about the Lord all the way to St. Louis. He spent the night there. The next day he sat by a man who talked about the Lord all the way to Oklahoma City. It went like that all the way to San Francisco.

When he arrived in San Francisco, he called his office and asked his Sergeant Major to call his wife. Tell her, I have quit smoking, quit drinking and swearing. (I didn't know he did any of those.) The Sergeant called and told her. Marguerite called me crying, she said," OH Chaplain, he is trying to be good enough to go to heaven and you know and I know you can't be good enough to go to heaven. You have to let the Lord save you."

I said, "Marguerite, dry your tears. we are claiming his salvation and we will see him saved.

She said, I don't think he will ever trust the Lord. You are going to Vietnam in about six weeks and I want you to promise me you will baptize me before you leave. I assured her I would baptize her in the river that runs through the heart of Indianapolis. I promised.

When we were talking about baptizing the couples he told her she had been baptized when she was a baby, why would she want to be baptized again? She tried to explain that she was a believer now and she wanted to have a believers baptism. He asked, "Have you ever seen any-one baptized by immersion? Let me tell you how it is. You will go down under the water, come up and your hair will be stringy, your clothes will be stuck to you. You will look horrible." He described it like it was the kiss of death.

She said, "Well, maybe so, but I want to follow the Lord in baptism and I don't care what I look like or what people think."

He said, "Well, I don't know what to think about you." That was not much of an encouragement for her to go ahead and be baptized.

Don returned from California, was pleasant as always , was pleasant with his wife. Sunday came and we had planned for baptizing Marguarite on Sunday afternoon. She had so wanted him to be ready to be baptized also but she would go ahead as it was the last chance for me to baptize her.

At three o'clock we gathered at the chapel and were waiting for all to get there, Don asked if he could talk to me and his wife alone. I unlocked my office and we stepped inside. He looked at me and with a smile, said, "Could you baptize two of us?" I asked if he was referring to the two couples in St. Louis. He said, "I am referring to you baptizing me and my wife this afternoon." Tears came to her eyes and a heavy look came over her face instead of a look of joy. She said, "I know you would do almost anything to please me but getting baptized won't take you to heaven."

He said, "I know how much the two of you have prayed and tried to get me to become a believer in the Lord Jesus Christ. I didn't tell either of you separately as I wanted to tell the two of you at the same time. In California I put my full faith and trust in the Lord." She grabbed him and hugged him and wept with joy. As she stood back he said, "Don't you remember this old suit that we were going to get rid of, I wore it down here today so it would be the one that got wet in the river." With rejoicing we went to the river.

I lead the way into the river as I had reconned before hand where it would be easiest to get into the water and found a place deep enough for the services. As we drove the cars to the spot, I thought, "Oh, no." Here were some hippies at the waters edge with bikinis on which were almost nothing. They were drinking beer and smoking pot while one was doing a passionate dance on a blanket. I didn't know what to do but I reached into my glove compartment and picked out some Christian literature and walked over to them as other cars drove up. I told them I wanted to give them something that is an eternal treasure on how to get to know the Lord, change their lives and eternal destiny. I handed them leaflets on salvation and forgiveness. They accepted them and were quiet. I was hoping it would last while we had services. I didn't ask them to leave as it was a public park. I walked out in the river, read Scripture verses, handed my Bible to someone on the shore and we three all walked out further together.

At that time a little boy about ten years old swung out over the river on a rope, dived in and came up right by me. I was in uniform and he said, "What are you doing out here with your Boy Scout Uniform on?"

I waded out into fairly deep water as Don Williams is quite tall. He looked at me and asked, "Really, can you baptize us together?" I had learned years ago as a young preacher if you are baptizing in running water, you lower them into the water up stream and as you raise them up the current helps lift them. I got them positioned right and told Don to bend his knees as they went down. He did and all went well. As we were wadding out of the water after prayer, the hippie types who had been on the blanket, started playing their guitar and singing, Shall We Gather At the River." They knew the verses all the way through. I knew they hadn't learned that song after we had arrived and they didn't have a song book there. They had been to church some time. I went over and thanked them for singing and asked where they learned that song? They hung their heads and said, "Chaplain, we grew up different than the way we are living and we know better than doing like we are. We are just glad we were here to see this." I took time to share with them before we left.

Don and Marguerite had already left but I went to Don's office on Monday morning to see how Don felt. Considering what a proper Army

Colonel he was about those hippies being at the river at such an important occasion for him. As he came up he said, "Good morning, wasn't yesterday great? You know what I thought about when those hippies were there? I thought, this is just what a baptism is suppose to be, a witness in the world, to the world, about the experience of dying to self and sin and being raised to walk in a new way of life with Jesus." I didn't have to say a thing. I just shook his hand and agreed. We worry too much about little circumstances that God has under control all along.

✝ 13 ✝

VIET NAM

Our time at Ft. Benjamin Harrison had ended, July, 1967. I wanted to take the family for a good vacation before leaving to Vietnam so we decided on attending Expo '67 in Montreal Canada. The two older children were gone, Mark to the Army and Beth, teaching school. Charlene and I, Steve and Crystal had a delightful trip to Montreal. On returning, we made our way to Kansas City where they were to stay while I was in Vietnam. When the time came for me to fly out early on a Sunday morning, I had a TWA flight to the west coast.

I had been told there was a fine Christian infantry officer who had been the Army representative to the civilian run Military Academy at Boonville, Missouri. A mutual friend had told me to be looking for him as he was going to Vietnam also. As we checked in we met Lt. Colonel. Ben Purcell. We got our families acquainted and after leaving the airport they went to church together.

Would you believe our seats were side by side so we had fellowship together on our trip! Of course we couldn't be in church so we read our Bibles and had a worship time together. As we finished praying, I looked out the window and right below us was the Air Force Academy Chapel in Colorado Springs, with the spires on top like fingers reaching into the sky. Even though we were at 30,000 ft. it was so clear, like a picture card photo. It was a good Omen that here we were above a building dedicated to the praise and glory of God. We looked at it and Ben said, "Do you know what I was praying for most of all? I was praying that no matter what else might happen to me, I did not want to be taken prisoner of an atheistic, oriental communist. They treat people so badly, especially if they know you are a Christian." I concurred with him.

We arrived in Travis Air Force Base and they put us on different planes for our trip on over to Vietnam. The trip was very uneventful. I was given one of the best assignments I could have had under the circumstances, that of being the chaplain for an Engineer Brigade with a General Officer commanding. There were about 18,000 hard working combat engineers. The only time they did any fighting was when they were attacked. I got to watch them build sea ports, rescue and recover things from the sea, build air fields with perforated steal planking or membrane like the inside of a tire that is laid down for a temporary air field or anything in between to include a concrete air field at An Khea that could take any kind of plane and even be used for a City Airport. We had "hot mix" companies that paved roads from the South, all the way to the border, through Da Nang and the Hi Van Pass. It was the most interesting time I could have had in a combat zone. Occasionally we had people blown up or shot but basically we were a working, building outfit.

The first Commanding General had just become a Christian and was so excited over knowing the Lord. He was replaced by a General from Dallas, Texas who was the most pleasant person you could ever work for. I thank God again for leaders like that in service. I remember going from where I stayed and walking over to the Generals Mess for meals. In the military, a "flag officer" has special things provided for his dinning facility. We ate off of china with regular flat ware. We were seated at tables with table cloths.

We were gone from our unit quite a bit, checking on our chaplains and units. I had 17 or more chaplains scattered around the country. A total of over 30 went through while I was there. One was blown up but not killed. He was medically evacuated out.

The rotation system made almost double the number of chaplains I was responsible for. Almost without exception, they were fine people. Early on in my tour of duty I had one come by as he was leaving country. I asked the General if he could eat at The General's Mess. He said, "More than that, he can eat at my table." The chaplain shared the things he had seen and done and the work his battalion had done that year. The General appreciated that and said, "I want every one of the chaplains, as they travel through for various reasons, to stop and spend the night. We have better living accommodations than where they are. Tell my aid and have them sit at my table. I think we can learn a lot from these men of God who have been troops out where the action is." This was a real blessing to the Chaplains. Most had never been around a General and here they were privileged to sit at his table in the Generals

Mess. It was a blessing also in that the word soon got out across the command that covered sixty percent of south Vietnam that the Chaplains were highly regarded by the Commanding General.

He also ordered his staff to always let me have a seat on his executive plane if I needed to go where he was going. He also told them, if he wasn't using the plane, it belonged to me. Every morning at the airstrip there was to be a helicopter for my use. He didn't assign a helicopter to me that may be down for maintenance. I was to have a flying, ready to go, aircraft every day. If I didn't need it I would tell them and they could release it for other use. I would never have asked for that kind of wonderful support and coverage but that is the kind we had and it made the mission so much easier for us.

During the tour I received a call one day from Chaplain Bill Bagnall whom we had been with several times. His room mate in their make shift bachelor officers quarters, was Infantry Lt. Colonel Ben Purcell. Ch. Bagnall said, "No names mentioned, but our dear mutual friend has just been shot down in his helicopter and taken captive by the Viet Cong. This was the second day of the Tet Offensive, 1968. Be praying that his life will be spared." At that time, Ben was the first senior officer that had been taken captive in South Vietnam by the Viet Cong. They tied his hands behind him and lead him through the villages with a rope around his neck like a dog, to show they were the conquers and here was a senior officer they had taken captive.

A long range patrol followed and watched through telescopes and binoculars but never found a time they thought they could recapture Ben and get him loose without getting him killed. You may remember in Readers Digest a condensed book section, "LOVE AND HONOR". That was a book written by Ben Purcell and his wife Ann. He was faithful to her, loved her, and planned his prison time life around her and his family.

Ann was told he was Missing in Action and presumed dead. I knew that wasn't so. I got word back to my wife to tell her we knew he was alive at that point. She was a burdened lady. Ben was taken to the North and when our prisoners were returned to us, Ben was on the very last plane out.

We have seen Ben at different times and he is now Congressman to his home state of Georgia. He is still going on with the Lord and a great patriot. He was in solitary as a prisoner for four years. Twice he escaped but being very fair skinned, light hair and blue eyes, he stuck out like a sore thumb in the orient. It was amazing they didn't shoot him when they recaptured him but they would take him back and put him in solitaire. They took his ring, watches and everything away from him. He scratched a calendar to keep track of time and marked each of his families birthdays, their anniversary and holidays. There in his cell alone, he celebrated those times for his family back home. This helped him maintain his sanity during those long years. God kept him and he still is faithful to the Lord. I say "Praise the Lord for a man like Ben Purcell," who really is a National Hero.

The tour in Vietnam went well and good things happened. I have already mentioned how I was visiting at Danang when Sergeant Green came up and shared how he had met the Lord when the Lord spared his life in the Delta two years before. Those are the things that bond military people together in a way no outsider could ever understand. That bond is doubled or tripled when it is cemented and covered over as icing on a cake by a Christian experience and a mutual understanding.

✝ 14 ✝

FORT HOOD, TEXAS

One evening when I went to my place at the table, there was a copy of 'Army Times' with a sheet of orders laying on top of it. It was orders assigning me to be Division Chaplains at Ft. Hood, Texas. I looked at the 'Army Times' and the headlines read, "Ft. Hood, or Ft. Head." There were so many drugs users, called 'dope heads', among the returnees from Vietnam that caused the headlines. They all laughed over the set up. I said, "I don't care what it is now, as God can change an entire fort."

Folks, God is still doing His thing around the world and if we don't get in His way, He will most certainly bless us.

I reported to Ft. Hood without taking any leave as I had been told by Washington I was needed there right away. I didn't understand why. By this time it was August, 1968. If you remember there were riots in Chicago and it looked as if the whole city might go up in flames while the Democratic Convention was being held there. Ft. Hood was on alert to go to Chicago and ring that city with soldiers to return peace to it under Marshall Law if something happened like it did in Los Angeles years later. We had soldiers flown into Great Lakes and Navy Stations around Great Lakes, ready to move in to save the city in case it was needed.

When I arrived at Ft Hood, signing into the First Armored Division, just before midnight, they told me there was a meeting going on to decide which chaplains would fly up to be with the men to pacify the city of Chicago. That was my reception to Ft. Hood, Texas. I did not go but stayed to get acquainted. The chaplains had wonderful support from the Commanding Generals. The colors were replaced and we became the First Cavalry Division.

I had served with the First Cavalry Division in Japan years before so I put the patch on again. At this time the Commanding General was James C. Smith, an aviator as this was an Air Assault Division. He was a dedicated Christian man. He called me in and asked who was responsible for the spiritual life of this division. I looked him in the eye and said, "You are Sir." He said, "You know, most chaplains don't realize that. You are my specialist to help and advise me but I am responsible for the men of this division, whether they eat, whether they sleep, whether they are doctored, and whether their souls are in good shape." I greatly respected that man and we made a great team.

I knew our work was cut out for us. First of all, there were one hundred and forty black soldiers who refused to get on the plane to fly to the Chicago area. They were all court marshaled. Most were not given very heavy sentences but it took two years to finish court marshaling all the men who sat down on the pavement and would not get on the planes. That was happening the very hour I reported for duty at Ft. Hood.

I said to our chaplains, "I want you to find out who any men are in this group who are from your unit, and are in the stockade awaiting court martial. I want you to visit each one of them at least once a week and if they need you any more often, visit them more. This was a matter of conscious with them as it was principally the blacks in the inner city that caused the uprising and they felt they could not come across a black brother. I told them I didn't care what their back ground was. All but two of our chaplains were Caucasian but I wanted them to all visit the soldiers until we found out what their future held.

I personally, over the next several weeks, visited each of the one hundred and forty men. I wanted them to know, although they were in trouble, there were people in responsible places that still cared for them.

It came the end of January, 1969 and they were still sorting out what the people's thinking was and what should be done to them. At that time Martin Luther King's birthday was not a national holiday. The Commanders didn't know just what they should do for his birthday so the Three Star, Corps Commander, a very fine gentleman, Beverly Powell said, "Until we get word from higher headquarters we will not have celebrations by any one.

I was having a Sunday evening service just before his birthday and suddenly I heard sirens coming from every direction on that post. They had called all military police on duty to come to the stockade. The stockade had TV in each barracks and they had a prearranged plan, when a certain program ended they kicked the TV tube out, threw all of the white prisoners out the window without bothering to open the windows. It didn't matter if it was first floor or second floor. They were laying there with broken bones, bruises and cuts. No one could go to them to help them. They had certain ones designated to overcome the guards. The black prisoners had taken charge of the military stockade.

I knew from the sirens something serious was going on so I quickly dismissed the services and headed for the trouble spot. I had a black Chaplain, Joel Miles. I thought a lot of Joel and I knew the prisoners knew and trusted him as he had been having services for the stockade. I knew every prisoner there had heard of him and maybe half of them had attended his services. I called him to come help and also another black Chaplain who had just arrived, Chaplain Matthew Zimmerman. While I was doing this the Full Colonel Provost Marshall showed up and said, "I'm going in there with a bull horn and give the orders. I'll then tell them what to do."

I said, "Sir, that is exactly what we need. They would like to have a Senior Officer go in there and taken hostage to use as a bargaining tool. We don't need that at all. Will you let me try to resolve this thing peacefully instead of having a shoot out?" I was a Lt. Colonel. I hadn't been there very long and we hadn't really met as he was at the Post side and I was Division. He looked at me and since he wasn't quite sure what he was doing anyway he said he would give me a quick try to do something.

We had a black Chaplains Assistant Bob Bohner, who was a tremendous musician. He could hear the first line of a song and pick it up and go on the piano. He could sing all the way from baritone to soprano. Bob Bonner was a fabulous young man, from the inner city of Chicago. I said, "Bob Bonner, the musician and Joel Miles, the Chaplain will go in and play and sing."

The Provost Marshall said, "Now you know our three Star Boss has said there will not be a Martin Luther King service." I said, "They aren't going in there for a service, they are going in there to sing. If I understand right, these black soldiers love to sing and they will gather in the chapel just to sing. They aren't all bad, some had nothing to do with this but they are in charge as all of the gates and doors are open internally. We can hear the singing."

Joel Miles was the officer responsible but the young black enlisted man from Chicago, was the man that saved the day. He began playing the organ and singing. The prisoners began to sing with him and they packed the chapel out. It was a warm Sunday evening there in Central

Texas and the room was so full they began to sweat. They sang loudly and burn up energy. After about an hour and a half things had become quiet. No windows were being broken or other destruction. Bob Bonner began to play and sing Aaaaaaamen, Aaaaamen. He sang that for about five minutes and I turned to the other officer and said "There's the benediction folks. They have sang down to a peaceful moment and everyone is going to go back to their cells." Sure enough they peacefully went back to their appointed places, the guards went in and there were no more problems.

They had to live without windows for awhile until they could repair the damage that was done. The uprising was resolved without anyone being shot or tear gas being used, simply by singing Christian hymns. The power of the Name of the Lord changes things. It changed the riot and turned it into a peaceful night.

The back up Chaplain for Joel Miles that I mentioned, was Matthew Zimmerman who just recently retired as the Army Chief of Chaplains. He was the first black minister serving as a Chaplain in any service to wear a Star. He retired as a two star General. We had from God's resources, the answer to man's problems. I believe God's resources are always the answer to man's problems.

One of the most touching experiences I observed in the three full years that I was Division Chaplain at Ft. Hood. Our chaplains worked so hard and did such good work. One day I was flying out to a training area with General Desobry, our second Commander. One of our Chaplains was out there with the troops. He talked to him awhile and on the way back in the helicopter he said, "Jim, we are going to have a Division Parade in honor of the Chaplains and the good work they are doing." I said "General Desobry, I appreciate the thought but Chaplains should not work for earthly honor, they should work as a Servant of God. Their rewards are spiritual and from the Lord. I would rather you didn't do that." He looked at me in a way I knew what it meant as my Commanding General speaking, he said, "Now, I have already decided I am going to do it. I am talking to you about the details."

I knew it was not open for discussion. We had the parade and all of the Chaplains were out front and were honored by the colors and guidons of the units of that Division. Pictures were made and the Public Information Officer wrote a story that was to go to 'Army Times.' I knew him personally. I asked him to give me all of the stuff that was suppose to go to 'Army Times' to be spread world wide about Chaplains being honored here at Ft. Hood. He asked why and I told him I really didn't want it to be noised abroad world wide. We consider it an honor to be serving with a Godly man such as General Desobry and with this outfit. We don't want other chaplains around the world to think we are trying to find glory for ourselves. He gave it to me and I still have it today.

General Desobry would mention from time to time, wondering when our Chaplains story was going to be distributed. Of course, it never was. I will be sending him a copy of this book and here it is over twenty five years later, he will finally find out what happened to the story. May I say in this paragraph, "General, forgive me, but I just felt like Chaplains should be humble servants of the Lord. I thank you for honoring us and giving us that kind of attention but we were rewarded enough in serving the Lord and serving you, as our Commanding General."

✝ 15 ✝

A Duty Day for God

Each year for several years, there had been a four week time frame in early Spring that Ft. Hood had what was called, 'A Duty Day for God,' which had been started by General Ralph Haines. This was a day a soldier could attend a retreat type service all day but it was counted as a Duty Day. It was, but it was for God. The whole post had engaged in this program in 1969 and 1970. It was coming up for 1971 and I knew it would be my last year there so I volunteered to be the project officer to run the 'Duty Day for God.' I wanted to make it a more meaningful 'man meeting God' experience than I had seen it be. When I volunteered to do all of the work for it, they were glad for someone to take the responsibility. I am talking about a post with fifty to sixty thousand soldiers on it. Things really had to be scheduled. We had seven different places that had Catholic services every day and the same had Protestant services. That went on for the whole month of February.

I started planning ahead in the summer of 1970 for the February, '71 'Duty Day for God' experience. I needed to find out how much money I would have for the project to bring in resource people. I knew something about how to get money from the military, as I had taken courses that Comptrollers, who handle the military money take at Ft. Benjamin Harrison, which is the Army finance Center. I had obtained quite a bit of money but still didn't have quite enough to do all I really wanted to. For instance, we had a special gathering of all the Senior Sergeants of the post. We brought in a famous foot ball player, Bill Glass, who now has a prison ministry for a luncheon. He really challenged these men to be 'men of God, as leaders'.

For the Senior officers we brought in the Chief of Chaplains to be the speaker. We had a special retreat for those who were Full Colonels or Generals. The invitation went out on the Commanders stationary. There is something about exclusiveness that fascinates people. We had a good turn out. When it came time to come to the altar to pray, no one moved. The three star General stepped out and came to the altar and said, "I don't know about the rest of you here but I am a man that needs God more than I have him and I am going to pray here and be prayed over." At that point, nearly everybody came to the altar to be prayed for as the Leader had lead the way in humbling himself before the eyes of men and women. Their spouses were there with them.

We were trying to cover every level of the military operation. There was a nineteen year old young man attending college in Waco. He was on TV giving his testimony. The program was simply called, "A Boy Named Steve." He was telling how he had been a junkie on drugs. He was also telling them how he was delivered from drugs and the horrors that they can get you into. He was a large man and he had a girlfriend who was not very large and was not on drugs. She kept saying, "If drugs are so good, why don't you mainline some drugs for me?" He had mixed the same dosage that he, as an addict, would take, who weighed about twice as much as the girl friend. After giving her that dose, she was brain dead in a hospital near by. I signed a contract with Steve. He would attend college in the morning and come every afternoon in the month of February.

We had tremendous speakers coming but I still wanted to do a major 'kick off' to start that month. I got in touch with Pat Boon but of course he was under contract with a public relations department that handled all of his business. For him to sing a couple of songs and give a short testimony of how he came to know the Lord, they wanted all expenses to bring him there and back plus two thousand and six hundred dollars. I had run out of money by then but I had met some Christian business men in Killeen. One of them said they were getting ready to open a new mall and if he will come by, walk up on the platform and wave at the crowd before cutting the ribbon, "we will pay all expenses of bringing Pat Boone to our city and you can have him for your kick off night at Ft. Hood." The Lincoln dealer provided a uniformed chauffeur in a new Lincoln Town car. They went first class in a manner that we could be proud of.

Following the kick off night which was so crowded out everyone couldn't get in, we had a reception for him at our house for the Generals and ladies and those who had made it possible, to personally meet Pat Boone.

By the time the 'Duty Day for God' started the next Monday morning, the post was excited over attending. With all of the plans needed for the February meeting, I had started in the summer before preparing. In November of 1970 I was in the bedroom on my knees praying that the details of February would begin to fall in place under the Hand and the Spirit of God. While praying, I was having interference from my nose as my wife was in the other end of the house baking brownies. I stopped praying, to decide if I would continue or go to the kitchen for brownies and milk. While I was quiet there on my knees, God spoke to me. He said, "While you are having the meeting in February, you will receive a call from Washington, telling you they are going to send you back to Europe." I waited but that is all God said. I was excited because we like Europe.

I got up from my knees, went to the kitchen for brownies and milk and said to my wife, "God told me in February, we are going to be alerted to go back to Europe." We discussed it but one of our concerns was that our youngest daughter, the only child left at home, was a Junior in High School and we would go to Europe and change schools for her Senior year. We talked about it with her and we said, "God knows what He is doing and our life belongs to Him so whatever He wants, we will do." We believe He controls our assignments and up until now He has done a good job of running our affairs. We rested it with Him and wondered where we would be assigned in Europe.

The next day our daughter came home from school and told us that at the end of the year, she would only lack one course to graduate. They had a system in the Killeen High School that it could be taken by extension so she could graduate in May and be free to stay in America and go to college. We realized God really was in this by not even disturbing our daughter's schooling.

✠ 16 ✠

TROUBLE IN VIET NAM

I made it a practice every morning to leave the house well ahead of regular duty hours and going by the Military Police desk as well as by the Duty Officer's desk and read the reports. This would give me all of the intelligence of what had happened since yesterday to anyone on the post. I was in my office by seven o'clock even though duty hours didn't begin until seven thirty. I would have time to call any chaplain who may need to see someone in the emergency room or for other needs. This would keep them from being surprised by some commander who wanted to know if their need had been taken care of. This was a help to the Chaplains and I felt it was my duty as the Division Chaplain over them.

I had gone to the office early and the phone rang. My wife told me a Chaplain friend in Vietnam had called our home, thinking I would still be there. He would be ringing my phone in a minute. Our youngest son, who at that time was still only eighteen years old, was in Vietnam. He had volunteered and gone over the day he was eighteen from Korea. He had been in Vietnam just about a year.

The phone rang and it was the Chaplain in Vietnam. He said, "Jim, if you want to see your son alive you are going to have to get to Vietnam. There has been a terrible incident and he is in the middle of it all. I don't know if he is going to survive." I asked some questions about it and what had happened was, there had been a shoot out between blacks and whites in the army in Vietnam.

If you saw the movie, "Platoon" you know some of the terrible things that happened. Let me add though, about the movie, 'Platoon'. The worst things that happened in ten years time were compressed into two hours of a terrible movie. It wasn't that bad every day, all day for ten years. That is not so. There were times it was that bad for awhile. I hung up and called my wife to share with her.

From my office I could look out my window and about four blocks away, see the headquarters for our division. The Commanding Generals Office was on the end of the headquarters toward my building. I could look out and see when his lights were on, indicating he was there. When the lights came on I went over to see my Commander, General William R. Desobry, the very fine general I referred to earlier. I went in and told him I had a very disturbing call from Vietnam and I was going to take the day off and go home and be with my wife. He wanted to know the particulars and then said, "I think you should go to Vietnam." He rang the buzzer that brought his Adjutant General in who issued orders and took care of paperwork for him. He said, "Joe, cut orders for Jim to go to Vietnam." I knew he didn't have the authority to cut orders for me to go there.

I knew that only the Pentagon could authorize people to come and go to Vietnam, whether on a permanent change of station for a year or whether on a temporary visit. Lt. Col Quest also knew this and said so but General Desobry, in a very soft spoken way, said, "Joe, I know that." Col Quest asked what would be the authority for those orders. The General said, "You just heard me say it. The Verbal Orders of the Commanding General, VOCO is the authority."

Col. Quest answered, "Well you know that sense it effects something outside of your command I will have to send a copy of them to Washington and you will be in trouble."

The General, again very softly said, "Joe, I know that but I also know you don't have to send them for 45 days and Jim will be back from Vietnam then and we will just tear them up. Jim, you go on home and pack and Joe will bring you your orders."

I said, "General, I wouldn't ask you to do this as it might jeopardize your getting your third star and you deserve to be a three star General."

He answered me, "You didn't ask me to do this. I did this on my own. Now you go and get packed because if you were sitting at my desk instead of where you are, and I needed this kind of help you would give it. Well, I am going to give you the help you need."

You can tell how much I respect a man like that. I had emergency status for that leave. The only man I know of in that ten year war that went to Vietnam on emergency leave. Many come back for emergency leave but not over because of a son.

I won't tell his story for him, he has shared it in groups and someday he may decide to make it known but God restored the will to live in that young man. When I got there in the afternoon and went to see him he couldn't believe it was me. The next morning when I saw him he said, "Dad, I thought I had hallucinated or imagined you were here, but you really are here, aren't you."

I said, "Yes, son and I am going to be here for awhile. " I stayed fifteen days and checked into things that were going on that shouldn't have been. I was able to rebuild his strength and confidence inside as that is what really keeps us alive.

I had to return then as the 'Duty Day for God' was beginning as it was the start of February. I didn't have priority so it took me three days to get back to Ft. Hood, Texas. I got there the day Pat Boon was to be with us that night. I was groggy as I hadn't been to bed for three days and nights when we started the months special services.

✝ 17 ✝

EUROPE

As the very special month was progressing, I would have to swing by my office each day to check on the ordinary ongoing business. Just before lunch one day as I was pulling into my parking place, my Sergeant stuck his head out the door and said, "Washington is on the line, they want to talk to you."

I hurried in to answer the call which was the personnel officer for the Chief of Chaplains. He said they just wanted to alert me that they wanted me to go to Europe in the summer. This was the call the Lord had told me about in the October before.

He said, "Your last tour over seas was Vietnam and you have been in Ft. Hood three years so it is time for you to move. We want you to have a good tour with your wife and family in Germany but you know things aren't the best there now. Soldiers there have been to Vietnam and are unhappy, they have brought drug habits back with them from the Far East and we are short on Junior Sergeants who live and work right with the men so leadership isn't what it should be in day to day ongoing things. There are serious problems with drugs and race riots in US Army Europe. If you decide you don't want to go there, we will assign you to Alaska, Panama or some good place where you can have your family."

I realized I couldn't tell him I already knew this from the Lord as he didn't believe in dreams and visions and the Lord talking to us. I said, "OK, I'll talk it over with my wife and call you back in about three days with our decision." I already knew what I had to do. I had to do what God wanted and that was, go to Europe.

At home that night my wife and I rejoiced in that we had received the call the Lord had told us was coming. I called back in three days and told him it was fine, we would be glad to go there. They thought it was all done in the natural. Most of my life has been lived in the 'supernatural'. That's the way I want to live. I believe when a person is born again they become alive spiritually to God and God and His actions are above natural things. We are suppose to begin to flow with him. That is in the realm of the supernatural. What is every day business with God is supernatural for man kind. We returned for a second tour to Germany for a very fruitful tour of duty.

Our departure from Ft. Hood was a grand thing. We had been there for three years and knew so many fine people. We had moved in the Spirit for things of the Lord. They had farewell dinners, farewell deserts in the early evening, farewell breakfasts and luncheons. When we left for Europe we were almost dead from the excitement of the farewell from our many fine friends at Ft. Hood, Texas.

I had been told my pin point assignment before I got there. I was to be at Grafenwohr, Germany, the largest training area in all of Europe. It was where Hitler had trained his troops to fight World War II. I found out later that was not where they had wanted me. They had planned for me to be the Fifth Corps Chaplain in Frankfurt, Germany. A board had already met on my birthday, July 20, and I had been selected to be a Full Colonel but I would not be promoted for a year later when my name came up on the list for promotion. There was not a single Full Colonel senior priest in a senior job in Europe. The senior Chaplain there, was the Headquarters for all US Army Europe, Chaplain. The Catholics had protested this strongly enough they put a priest in Fifth Corps and sent me to Grafenwohr. I knew none of this until over a year later. I very happily went to my assignment.

I stopped in Washington in route to Europe to see my long time friend who had been a Major when he called me out of a class room and told me my family had been in a wreck some eighteen years before. He was now being promoted to two star Chief of Chaplains. He said to me, "Jim, the board has met and they haven't announced their findings but you will be a Full Colony." I said, "Thank you Sir but I am enough of a soldier that when it is in print, approved by Congress and signed off on by the President, then I will believe it." He said, "But I am telling you now. We will see who is right."

We arrived in Rhine Maine Military Airport in Frankfurt, Germany, just before midnight.

We had stayed in touch with a long time friend, retired Chaplain Louie Miller. He is interested in old Bibles and he has a better collection than the American Bible Society or the International Bible Society has. He had told us months ahead of time he was going to Europe and look for old Bibles. He planned to buy a Volkswagen camper model bus. As he and his wife traveled around they could stop and rest or even sleep in it for the night. He was planning to return to the states about the time we were to arrive in Germany so plans were made for him to meet us and we would buy the Volkswagen from him. He was a very conservative man and I knew the auto would be like new after he had used it for three months. When we arrived at midnight he met us and the next morning we went out to look at the bus and sure enough, it was just like new. We went over and changed the papers on it and we proceeded to Grafenwohr. I checked with the authorities at the Air Base and found out I could drive the Volkswagen as it had Belgian license on it, since I was on leave, but as soon as I signed in it wouldn't be legal. I showed them my leave papers and they said, "fine." God put it all together for me to be able to drive while I got the papers changed and insurance coverage.

The Chaplain we were replacing at Grafenwohr had already rotated and I wanted to be there as soon as possible. I had called Washington to see if they would change my orders to August instead of September as my orders read. They said there would just have to be a long gap and Grafenwohr could be without a Chaplain for awhile. I knew I could take a months leave, not use all of the leave and go on to Germany and sign in. A soldier can always go back to duty and not use his leave. I did that and arrived almost a month sooner than they were expecting me.

When we arrived we found out things were so bad, drugs so plentiful, that between the main camp and the five field camps, where the training for artillery, tanks etc. did their annual training and testing, we would get up in the morning and see if there were blood trails on the paths going back to camp. Blood trails from soldiers knocking another soldier in the head or knifing him, taking his money or his drugs. It was a horrible condition. That is what Washington had meant when they said I didn't have to take this assignment in Europe. Things are bad over there.

I went to the Commander and said, " "Sir, we are going to change this instillation. I believe any place a soldier is assigned, his own living area, should be one of the safest places on earth. If he is in combat, yes, we understand that his life is at risk but not in a place that is not suppose to be combat. It is mortal combat for soldiers to move around on this big Kaserne during the hours of darkness. We are going to change that."

He said if I could help him do it, he would be glad. I said, "Sir, I think God has sent me here. I want to tell you something. The devil is having his way here in this Kaserne." He wanted to know what I would suggest that we could do to overcome the situation.

I said, "I am a bit of a mystic. I believe in angles, I believe in demons, and I believe in a personage that is a superior military being, to all other spirit beings except to God Himself. I believe we are going to break the power of the enemy in the following ways. At the chapel, we will read the Bible through in seventy two hours, Friday, Saturday and Sunday, out loud over the post public address system. We are going to have prayer around the clock for seventy two hours. We will break the power of the enemy over this place and we will begin to have a safe post again." He said if that is what I thought would happen, we would do it.

We had a few complaints as some people said they didn't believe in the part of the Bible we were reading, or that we don't believe in the Old and New Testament as a Holy book but in a time of emergency, Commanders can do things that normally wouldn't be done. He said to those complainants, "When the power of evil is broken over my post, then we won't do things like this as a routine thing but right now my Chaplain says this is the way to loose the power of God and break the power of the devil and we are going to do it."

Almost immediately, the climate, morally and spiritually, changed on that camp. We didn't have to go out in the mornings and look for blood trails of the soldiers who had been attacked. Soldiers didn't have to be afraid at night to come into the main camp to go to the exchange or to chapel services or to get a meal. They didn't have worry about going back to go to bed in their own unit at night. The power of the enemy was broken by the power of The Word of God, the power of prayer and the power of The Holy Spirit.

✝ 18 ✝

THE MARVELOUS WORK IN KELLY BITKER

When I arrived in Grafenwohr, and was still putting things into my desk when the secretary said there was a young soldier waiting outside that needed to see me. I stopped and had Kelley Bitker come in. I told him to sit down and tell me why he needed to see a chaplain.

He said, "Chaplain, I am really in trouble. I am being court martialed, I have been on drugs, I have been worshipping Satan. I am probably going to be thrown out of the Army." He had on a warlock ring at the time. His wife and baby had gone back to Detroit. He said, "I don't know how I got in so much trouble." I asked what trouble he was in and he said he had been an Army mail clerk. There has to be a customs declaration made on items of value shipped through an Army post office back to America, so he knew if it was a three hundred dollar camera or a hi-fi set worth a lot of money. He stole them and sold them on the German black market. He had two hundred and forty three charges and specifications against him. He expected to go to prison for the rest of his life.

I said, "Kelly, your problem isn't legal. Your problem is spiritual, and there is a God in heaven who changes sinners like you." I began to read the scriptures to him. No one had ever done that before. He had been counseled by another Chaplain, he had two lawyers working on his case, his commander wouldn't let him pull any duty as they were afraid he would steal again. I went to the core of the problem and I read scriptures to him. In a couple of days, Kelley Bitker was a born again, Christian man.

I turned him over to the Youth With A Mission young people that they might mentor him scripturally and spiritually. We had him in our home and taught him to pray morning and night. We taught him to pray before he ate his meals, and to thank God who is the source of everything we have. This man grew by leaps and bounds. Youth with a Mission took all of his satanic warlock jewelry to the motor pool and with a cutting torch, cut it in pieces and buried it in the ground. He was delivered from the curses he had brought upon himself by living an ungodly, drug filled and illegal thievery life.

Finally the time came for his trial which cost thousands of dollars. They brought the soldiers who had been stolen from all the way from America, Vietnam, Alaska and Panama. The charges were brought against him and the last day of the trial with Germans there who had testified against him and were now released to hear the final arguments of the trial. I was brought in. His two lawyers had asked me to appear as a character witness, saying, "He says he has become a Christian under your teaching and that you know him now to be a God fearing, upright man." I agreed to testify.

I was brought into court and put under oath. They asked if I knew the accused, Kelley Bitker. I pointed to him and said, "Yes, that is Kelley Bitker." I was there for the defense and told them that I knew him to be a man of sound character. I know he is a God fearing and honest man. A ripple went through the court. The judge banged his gavel for order in the court. The people there knew he had stolen at least two hundred and forty three times.

When the defense lawyers had finished setting the stage for what they wanted me to do, the trial attorney came up and asked, "What do you mean, Kelley Bitker is an honest man? We have proven in this court his record of stealing. The court knows this, the judge knows this." I said, "Here is what I know about Kelley Bitker, he has been born again and the old man is not there. He is a new man." They said, "Do you mean he is a psychiatric case, do you mean he is schizophrenic?"

I said, "That's not what I mean at all. the Bible says when a man is in Christ Jesus, old things have passed away and behold all things are made new. This is a new man that is here. He is not the same man who stole all of those things. Again a ripple went through the court room and the judge again banged on the gavel. For an hour or more that trial attorney gave me a hard time but I set there and answered with the Word of God. Finally he had to quit and the judge recessed the court for one hour, after which the sentence would be pronounced. Everyone departed and the judge asked me to follow him to his chambers.

When we got to the chambers the judge said, "Chaplain, you may be wondering why I let that trial attorney give you such a hard time for an hour or more." I said, "Frankly, Your Honor, I was beginning to wonder." He said, "I'll tell you why I did it. I am a Christian too and there were two hundred and fifty or more people out there leaning forward listening to you. Their defenses were down and the Gospel was soaking into all of those people like they probably had never heard it before so I let it go on an undo amount of time. The judge hugged me and I hugged him. He told me I could go and come back in an hour to hear the sentence. I walked out of there thinking, 'God knows how to run His business.'

We reconvened after that hour of recess. If Kelly was sentenced to a year or more, he would be sent back to Ft. Leavenworth Disciplinary Barracks. Not the Federal Prison which is also located at Leavenworth, Kansas. If he was sentenced for less than a year, he would serve his sentence at the new Army Stockade near by at Nuremberg. The judge told the accused to stand and Kelly stood, not knowing what he was going to hear. The Judge said, "I sentence you to six months at the Nuremberg prison. There was not a ripple of expression or disbelief went through that court because they had understood that the accused was not the same man that had stolen things from them. The court was dismissed and they silently walked out of that court room.

I went over and said to Kelly, "God has indeed blessed you, young man." Kelly was taken immediately and locked up at the stockade in Nuremberg, Germany, the same city where the Nuremberg trials were held for the war crimes that were committed in World War II.

The story of Kelly Bitker doesn't end there. Chaplain Richard Johnson was the prison Chaplain. He was a good man but at the close of the duty day he went by the bar for a drink and to smoke his pipe with his fellow officers. His church denomination did not object to this.

When Kelly got to the prison, he was locked in his cell for seventy two hours, which was normal procedure, to see if he would go into depression or maybe even make an attempt on his life. This was for his own protection.

In that prison were people who were going to have longer sentences than a year, while waiting trial. Some were being held for murder or other violent crimes that they were accused of. They were not all non-violent like Kelly.

After the first day, Kelly said, "This is boring sitting here, isn't there some work I can do?" He was told he had to stay there for seventy two hours for the transition period. He said, "Well, I'm not going to do anything wrong, if you will just give me some work to do I would be glad. I've talked to some of the other prisoners and they say there is a chapel here. Would it be possible for me to clean the chapel?"

The Sergeant talked to the Confinement Officer and they decided if he wanted to, that it would be all right so he was allowed to clean the chapel. Now Kelly Bitker had not only been saved, he had been Spirit-filled. He knew how to do spiritual warfare. He knew how to pray down the anointing of God and his Holy Spirit on that place. Kelly cleaned the chapel as it had never been cleaned before. On his hands and knees he cleaned the base of the pews, he cleaned around the edges of the carpet. As he did, he laid hands on every piece of furniture there and prayed, "God, this is supposed to be Your place. The people that sit in this pew are suppose to be blessed of You." There were kneelers on those pews for the liturgical and he even dusted around the hinges. "God, when people kneel here, hear their prayers more than they expect. Change their hearts and lives." He prayed over every wall, the pulpit, everything there was blessed by God.

In the course of that, he met Chaplain Johnson and told him, "You know the evenings are boring here and you are in your office in the day time but if you would get it arranged, I would be glad to clean your office and dust all of your books at night when you are out." He went there at night while the others had free time. He dusted every book and shelf, desk and chair there, praying over each one as he did. He prayed for the anointing of God to fall on it. The next day he was on a different detail but Chaplain Johnson was in his office.

Chaplain Johnson told me this story himself. "I went in my office and as the day went on, there was a sense of the presence of God like I had never felt. The thought came to me, maybe I should pray." He was a liturgical and not in the habit of praying except out of the Prayer Book. "I am used to kneeling down to pray so I went over and locked my door so no one would come in and find me by my desk praying." Isn't it strange that a man of God should not want anyone to catch him kneeling in prayer? Shouldn't we think it very natural that people should find us from time to time on our knees before the Lord? But that is where this chaplain was at that time.

Kneeling on the chair he normally sat in, not really knowing how to pray, he began by saying, "God," and he stopped there, not knowing just how to proceed. He had never prayed a conversational prayer. Something tapped him on the head and he jumped up, thinking someone had entered the office and found him praying. No one was in the room and he checked the door. It was still locked. He thought this was very strange. He went back and knelt down as before. Again, something tapped him on the head. He now realized it was God and it was all right to talk to God in a conversational way and that God was listening. He poured out his heart to God and got saved and filled with the Holy Spirit. Why? Because a prisoner had anointed the chapel, the office, the desk, and the very chair he knelt by and the Holy Spirit was there. When he prayed, the Spirit of God had caused him to hunger and feel a need for prayer. God was there waiting for his prayer.

That is a wonderful story about Kelly Bitker but even that is not the end of the story.

A little later there was a riot in that prison and some of the worst criminals there had overpowered the guards and got the keys. They unlocked the cells and every prisoner was released from his cell. The alarm was sounded and a whole battalion of Military Police surrounded the prison. The Chaplain was called and he was outside. The Confinement Officer was there with an electronic bull horn. He called to them, "We have this place surrounded. No one is going to escape."

It was quiet for awhile and then a voice called out, "This is Kelly Bitker. My door is unlocked but I am still in my cell. I want you to give me a few minutes before you storm this prison. I want to go out and talk to them and get them to surrender."

They said, "No, some of these men are murderers, they are violent. They won't listen to you. You will just get hurt."

He answered, "No, Everybody here knows me. Everywhere I've gone, whether it is the mess hall or a work detail, ,I've told them I am a Christian and Jesus is the Lord and Savior of my life and I am going to obey His orders. They know what kind of a man I am but I want you to give me permission to leave my cell. I won't leave without your permission.

The Chaplain, who had this marvelous spiritual experience because Kelly had prayed over his place, said to the Major Confinement Officer, "Kelly is not an average prisoner, he isn't an average soldier, and I think you should give him permission to go out and talk to the ring leaders.

The Major said, "Chaplain, on your word I will give him a little time." I forget the number of minutes he told Kelly he could have but when the time was up, Kelly came back to the window and said, "It is all right now, they have returned to their cells and have given the keys and guns back. The guards can come out now. They will be calling you in a minute to tell you it is all over."

In a few minutes, the guards notified them that it was all under control. They went in and everyone was back in their cells. No one had been hurt and they sent all of the added police home.

The Chaplain and Confinement Officer took Kelly into their office and asked him what had happened. He simply said, "I went out there in the name of the Lord. I wasn't fearful for my safety. I told them, "Men, you are only getting yourself in more trouble. This is not what you ought to do. You need to submit to the authority over you. After they listened to me a little bit, that's what they did." They put Kelly back into his cell for the night.

The next morning they sent for him and said, "I have your uniform here. Get out of your prison garb and get into your uniform." The Confinement Officer called the Commanding Officer at Grafenwohr and told him to send a jeep to pick up Kelly Bitker as he was releasing him from prison.

The Commander said, "You can't do that, he was sentenced to six months and it has only been four weeks."

He was told, "You don't know what happened last night." and he told him the story. He said, "Of all the men here, this man is least of all supposed to be locked up in my place. I am releasing him now. There is no reason he needs to serve the rest of his sentence. If you don't send a vehicle after him, I will put him out on the autobahn to hitch hike home and he will be an embarrassment to your command." Soldiers aren't suppose to hitch hike in Germany.

The vehicle was sent and brought him back to our post, His Commander gave him the rest of the day off and he came to the chapel. I was surprised to see him. He told me the story and it was almost more than I could believe so I called down to Chaplain Johnson to verify it. He laughed and said there was more to the story than he had told. He said, "This man is a greater minister of God than I am."

He then told me about his own experience with the Lord. When it came the end of duty hours that day, he filled up his pipe and started over to the Officers club to have a drink, but he had been saved and filled with the Holy Spirit. "I started to light my pipe and my hand just wouldn't raise to light it. I thought it strange, I could not light my pipe. I finally put that pipe back in my uniform pocket`, still filled with tobacco that had not been smoked." I thought 'something is going on, I cannot understand,' I had smoked for years. I got to the club and ordered a drink. I picked the drink up but could not put it to my mouth. "I set it back down and tried it again. Finally I left it setting there and walked to my quarters. Praying silently, I said, God, what is going on. I cannot smoke or take a drink? By this time I knew I could talk to God in my heart."

God spoke to me, "I have saved you and filled you with my Holy Spirit. Your body is a Holy Spirit container and I don't want anything unholy put inside you with My Holy Spirit."

Chaplain Johnson laughed and said, "Have you ever heard anything like that?"

I answered, "Yes, God did that to me when I was thirteen years old."

And that is the story of Kelly Bitker at Grafenwohr, Germany

✝ 19 ✝

CHRISTIAN COFFEE HOUSE

During the months from the time I received my alert to go to Germany in February, 1971, and the time I arrived there in August, the Lord had shown me several things about my tour there. He had said that many soldiers were really rebellious against the military, it's uniforms and their Commanders. They didn't want to be in service. The draft was still going on but by 1975 we were going to change from a draftee army to an all volunteer army. Soldiers who were drafted were resentful over what was happening in the military. There was a spirit of rebellion loose in America and it had crept into the military. Even before I knew where my assignment was to be, God had said, "I am going to send young people who belong to Me and are not in the military, to change what is going on in US Army Europe."

After I arrived in Grafenwohr I began to inquire and look for these young people. One day I looked out my office window and there was a large Mercedes crew cab truck with a closed in bed. It was probably a four or five ton truck with four doors. About nine young people climbed out of it and went around to the back and started unloading musical instruments. My heart leaped within me. I said, "This must be some of those young people who are going to help me break the power of the enemy over soldiers in US Army Europe." They stayed for two weeks going around holding services and many people were saved. I thought, surely, these are the ones God has sent. I prayed with them, I appreciated them, I loved them, they were from a Spirit filled church in Grand Prairie, Texas. I couldn't expect any finer people to show up to help me than they were. We all prayed and agreed that they were to go back to Grand Prairie.

I knew they weren't the ones God had sent. I inquired of other chaplains serving in Europe if they knew any young people that God has sent to Europe that might come help us win the souls and hearts of the soldiers here.

There was a Chaplain in Hanau, Germany who had served with me already three times. Paul Norris had reported to Ft. Benjamin Harrison, Indiana in 1967 for his first assignment as a Chaplain with his wife Pat and their two small sons. They now have four of the finest sons I have ever known. I was glad to know Paul, a graduate of a Presbyterian seminary in Texas. He had been in Vietnam when I was. While we weren't assigned together, we would go by to see each other. He considered me his mentor. He was with an Armored Cavalry outfit, in the forward edge of the battle at all times. He returned from Vietnam and served under me in the Division. He had departed ahead of me to Germany.

I called Paul in Hanau and asked if he knew any young people that might help me. He said he had a young man working for him that may be with a group that can. I went to see him and the young man had been with Youth With a Mission in the States and been drafted.

Thomas Bragg had been assigned to Europe instead of Vietnam as most of the draftees were. Tom told me about Youth With A Mission. They had started a coffee house in the basement of the chapel where Paul Norris was in Fligerhorst Kaserne, in Hanau, Germany. I visited their meetings and saw what they were doing. They were in civilian clothes, they had religious literature, Bible study, prayer times and ministry to the troops. Tom was leading the ministry and I liked what I saw. He said he could put me in touch with the leaders.

Loren Cunningham, the organizer and head of Youth With A Mission, had his headquarters in Lussane, Switzerland. The two brothers, Garry and Don Stevens, & David and Carol Boyd, all leaders were there. One night at Grafenwohr we received a call and Garry Stevens and David Boyd were in route. They were having trouble finding just how to get into Grafenwohr Kaserne and to our house. We talked and prayed with them and shared our situation. They said they would report to their leader, Loren Cunningham and would get back with me. In a matter of days, a Volkswagen bus found it's way to us with three people in it. A young man from England, one from Ireland, and a young lady from America

I went to the Commander and told him we needed these young people. He said we could have anything we needed. We opened a Christian Coffee House on post and the soldiers started getting saved. Here were young people like they wanted to be only they had been drafted into the Army. God used that to help change what was going on in US Army Europe.

We had a coffee house situated on this major training area for US Forces Europe, operated by the Youth With a Mission.

One snowy evening, my wife and I had been out for a walk and decided to stop in to see how things were going in the Coffee House. Normally we tried to have a low visibility presence there as there was a great deal of resistance by the draftees in the US Army during those days, against any military authority;. Sometimes I would go by and visit in civilian clothes to keep a high military presence from being known.

The house had been used as the station for dispatching train loads of soldiers to the front. We had the windows covered to about six feet from the ground so those outside could not look in. We had planned to have curtains on the top but had not yet put them in. As we approached the building, we heard loud voices. We stopped at one of the windows and I could see inside by standing on tip toe. My wife could only hear what was going on. As I looked inside, instead of the usual twenty or thirty soldiers and youth who helped with the operation, I saw only two Youth With a Mission men and one soldier.

The soldier, a large man, probably weighing over two hundred pounds and above six feet tall, would run to one end of the building and yell, "I'm going to worship Satan.' Then he would run to the other end and yell, "No, I'm going to worship Jesus,"

The two YWAM men, one from California and one from Ireland, were watching this, with needless to say, some degree of interest. The soldier repeated this a number of times and than ran up to the YWAM men and said. "NO, THIS IS IT, I am going to worship Satan." When he did he stiffened himself and leaned back on his heels and fell stiff as a board to the floor on his back with his head hitting the concrete floor. He laid there motionless.

The young man from California knelt down beside him, lifted one of his eye lids and his eyes were rolled back into his head.

I was shocked. I was responsible for the entire program of the Coffee Houses and here was a man that had struck his head hard enough on the concrete floor I thought he surely had broken his neck or fractured his skull or both.

The YWAM young man looked up at his colleague with a very serious expression on his face. At that moment, the young soldier, lying prone on the floor, without using his arms or legs, levitated, and without any assistance from anyone or anything, rose straight up in the air and stood on his feet. He turned and ran out of the building, down the sidewalk behind me. I stood transfixed, frozen in place from what I had seen.

I looked for my wife and she had only been able to hear all of the yelling and couldn't see, so she had gone home a couple of blocks away. I went inside and said, "What has happened here and where are the others?

I found out the others were outside, kneeling in the snow, praying. They knew that here was a challenging, satanic man that had challenged the power and authority of Jesus Christ. They had left two inside to minister to him and the rest of them were calling on the power of God.

This soldier had made his decision. He had come in with the statement, "MY god Satan, is stronger than your god, Jesus Christ.

We all got together, inside the building and had prayer before going on home. The next morning I received a call that a soldier had gone berserk in the morning formation. Six soldiers had wrestled him to the ground as he was plainly out of his mind. They had put him in a straight jacket and locked him in a room. I went to see him and it was no surprise that it was the same soldier who had made his vow to Satan the night before. He was med.-evaced back to Walter Reed Hospital, Washington, DC.

It is a wonderful thing to trust the Lord Jesus Christ and a terrible thing to be a follower of Satan. This man had made the choice and paid the price and his mind no longer belonged to him.

✝ 20 ✝

FRANKFURT

The Fifth Corps had fifty thousand soldiers under a three-Star General. They covered half of Europe for a tactical part of US Army Europe. The Senior Chaplain over Europe called and told me I was being moved to the Fifth Corps Headquarters in Frankfurt. I said "I really want to stay where I am, God is doing a great work and a revival is taking place. We are changing the soldiers who are coming here for training, from the different units from all over US Army Europe.

He said, "No, I am moving you to Fifth Corps. You are on the list for Colonel and I am putting you in a Colonels job." I didn't say much more but the next morning I got up before daylight and when he came into his office in Heidelburg, I was standing in the hall waiting. He said, "Good morning Jim." I said, "Good morning Earl. I've come to talk to you." He said, "You can talk to me about anything but your transfer. That is locked in concrete. You are going to Frankfurt. It's not open for discussion. Come in and have a cup of coffee and go back to Grafenwohr. You are moving there on the first day of July." This was May. I sat there, drank a cup of coffee, visited about little chit chat things, got in my car and drove back three hours to Grafenwohr.

By then we had about ten Youth With a Mission young people there and we were having meetings almost around the clock. I just did not want to leave. Soldiers lives were being changed and the Commander thought it was great. He had given them places to live as well as meeting places. I told them when they closed the Coffee House that night, I wanted those with Youth With a Mission to stay and we were going to have an all night prayer meeting. We prayed all night and the next day Earl called and said he had been up to Frankfurt and the General says he won't have you in his command."

I said, "That's wonderful, Earl. We had an all night prayer meeting and I think God has changed things." He said, "NO, he hasn't changed things. I'm getting your records together and I'm going back up there today to see him."

I said, "We are going to have another all night prayer meeting." He said I could do what I wanted to but I was going to Frankfurt. That night we had another prayer meeting and about three o'clock in the morning I was kneeling. They had hands laid on me. They had anointed me with oil. God said, "Read Ephesians 3:20, because that is how I am sending you to Frankfurt, Germany.

At that time I had not memorized Ephesians 3:20 and I said, "Stop praying for a minute. Hand me a Bible. I have to read the Word of the Lord." We give you that word now, in the text of this book. It says, 'Now unto him that is able to do exceedingly abundantly above all that we are able to ask or think.' God said, "That is what I am sending you to do for fifty thousand soldiers plus fifty thousand family members in that corps."

I said, "Folks, the prayer meeting is over. God has spoken." The next morning I went to my office and the phone was ringing. It was Earl Bloxom, a faithful man of God. He said, "I went down there yesterday, I was prepared to overcome the Generals arguments about your coming to his command and when I walked in he said, "Chaplain, I want Jim Ammerman and no one else as my chaplain. When are you going to assign him to my command?"

Earl said he almost staggered around, here he was to try to convince him and something had already changed his mind. The General said, "I have never met Jim Ammerman but he is the man I want." I then shared with him about God speaking to me at three o'clock in the morning so I would be happy to go to Frankfurt.

When I got to Frankfurt God began to move. One day I was alone with the General and I said, "Let me tell you about things that were going on down here and the things that were going on in the heavenlies about my coming to Frankfurt. I told him that story. He squinted one eye and looked at me, as he did when he was real serious and said, "Is that what happened?" He did not even know what had changed his mind. You see, God can change the mind of a man even though he doesn't know it. From that day forward, that very micro managing General never told me one thing to do but would ask me when he saw me, "What do I need to help you with."

That was the Chief of Staff who ran the Corps for a Three Star General, who was a God fearing Presbyterian. They had relieved the priest who had been sent there. He had already had his deputy, a fine Methodist, transferred. The Senior Sergeant had gotten out and returned to America early as there was a terrible fight going on in the Chaplain Section in V Corps. The chaplains had been praying for another leader so they could have some support and help.

When I reported in to the Commander, I had been at that headquarters for four days. I had hardly been to bed. I had read every paper in the files. There was a spiritual battle going on. I visited every Major Commander and every Senior Chaplain in the northern half of Germany in that four days time. The Commander was on leave when I arrived but on my fifth day there he was back and I reported in to receive the Commanders guidance. I had a fancy clip board with a cover that I flipped back as I walked up to his desk. I reported for duty and said, "I am here for your guidance for this Fifth Corps." He said, "I see you have some things on your clip board. Will you tell me what they are?"

I read off to him thirteen items I had learned in my visits. I said, "You may know about these things and you may not but here is what I have found. He knew only about half of them and wanted to know where I had been to learn all of this. I told him I hardly been to bed as I wanted to be of value to the command. He motioned me over to a divan by his desk and asked if I had received his briefing on racial relations and drug and alcohol abuse. He said, "Alcohol is a drug and it is damaging to the troops too. I am in an anti drug war and I don't even serve coffee in my office or allow people to smoke in my office or staff meetings. I am not going to have a young soldier to say 'why does some juice head sergeant or some tobacco smoking officer tell me I can't smoke pot or use other drugs when they are using drugs. I'm not going to have them throw those accusations back at me. We are going to win this drug war. What did you think of the briefing I had all officers receive on the war on drugs and race relations?"

I replied, "Sir, it's the finest program I have heard of, devised by the mind of man." He leaned back proudly in his chair and then I finished my statement, "doomed to failure." He quickly leaned forward and said, "What do you mean?" I said, "Sir, these are spiritual problems and there is no spiritual content in your program. They can only be won spiritually. I am here to help you win those battles but to do so we have to have a spiritual program."

He leaned back in his chair and thought for a minute before he came around from behind his desk and sat down by me on the divan. He said, "I have been an officer in the military for thirty three years. I have looked for a chaplain that could be my pastor for a third of a century and I think that this morning, I have found me a pastor. I can tell you are a man of conviction and I don't want you to ever be a 'yes man' on my staff. My door is open to you twenty four hours a day. Come in and tell me what you are hearing from God and we will take corrective action." We began to make plans that very hour that began to change, not only Fifth Corps but the other half of US Army Europe also.

After I had explained to the Commanding General that his drug alcohol program was doomed to failure because it didn't have a spiritual content to it, I knew I had better get busy and come up with an answer as to what would work. A good commander will insist, if you bring a problem to him, that you also bring an answer.

We decided we would rent some German retreat centers as well as the American ones and have a program that we termed, "The New Life Program." The Military likes two words to denote a program so we called it the New Life.

We would take the soldiers, who if they were any worse, they would be put out of the service. We would take them apart for a week, with one or two of our very finest, Godly Bible believing Christians and put them in charge. They would go somewhere for a week in a pleasant surrounding and lead these people to the Lord. They would return to their units where they served as so much better soldiers that the first sergeants began to call the Command Sergeant Majors at Headquarters about the New Life Program and tell him, "These duds that we gave to them, that we thought we could throw them out of the Army when they got back, have turned into good soldiers. They look good, they work good and they are obedient and well disciplined. We don't know what the Chaplains are doing to these men but they are different men."

At that point, we knew we had a program that would change anyone that wanted to be changed in US Army stationed in Europe.

I felt my wife and I should go to Switzerland and meet the man who was the head of the organization that was helping us so much, Loren

Cunningham, of Youth With a Mission. David Boyd, one of his right hand men had come to Frankfurt for me. I had him recon our needs with me. He said he would go back to America and recruit young people to come open coffee houses in every major installation in Fifth Corps. They will be the evangelism arm of the Chaplaincy. He got on a plane and flew back to America.

My wife and I drove to Laussane, Switzerland where they had taken an old 'Hotel by the Golf Course' and turned it into a training center there in the French speaking part of Switzerland.

When we arrived they fixed us some tea and Loren said, "Bring your tea, let's go in the office, I need to talk to you." Loren is a real man of God. His organization has more missionaries around the world than any other organization. He said, "I was praying for you and your work and God showed me a vision. He gave me some facts and figures in that vision. Loren did not know I had been praying for Bibles. I had an organization that would send me ten thousand New Testaments every three months. With a Corps the size we had, there were more people than that rotating every quarter and new ones coming to replace them. In effect, I was going backwards in placing the Word of God in the hands of the people. I had prayed for a complete Bible to put in the hands of every one of these hundred thousand people who will receive one. Because many are Bible illiterates, having never read the Bible, I wanted a simple, plain English translation. The King James was too hard for them. This had been my prayer for a number of weeks so I was ready to hear what Loren had to say.

He said, "Here is the vision God gave me as I was praying for you. God showed me truck loads of Bibles coming into Frankfurt for delivery to you. I don't know anything about the military needs but I know those trucks were loaded with Bibles. Not just New Testaments, they were complete Bibles. They were in the Living Bible Translation. I asked in that vision, 'how many Bibles are there.' I had no basis of knowing the numbers you needed but the Lord spoke to me and said, 'there are one hundred thousand Bibles." He stopped to see my reaction.

I said, "Praise God. I have been praying for simple translation Bibles and enough for the one hundred thousand Corps." We stood up and rejoiced because God had spoken to his servant, Loren Cunningham.

Loren said, "That's not all. I have never met Mr. Kenneth Taylor, who wrote that paraphrase of the Bible. I called a friend of mine in

America and asked if he knew how I can locate Mr. Taylor, head of Tyndale House Publishers. He said yes, and gave me the number. I called his office in Chicago and was told he was in the Middle East distributing Bibles in Moslem lands but he would be coming back through Frankfurt on his way home tomorrow and has a layover of two or three hours. I got the flight number and flew to Frankfurt to meet him."

He wasn't over a half hour from my house. He didn't call me or come see me. He set there in the airport with Dr. Kenneth Taylor, shared his vision, told him about the needs there and Ken Taylor said, "That's interesting Mr. Cunningham, I have a hundred thousand Living Bibles I am paying storage on in Murpheysburg, Tennessee. Dr. Billy Graham had thought he needed many more than he did and he had these left over. I will give them to Fifth Corps as soon as I get back to Chicago." They had a word of prayer there in that great airport that is called the 'Gateway to Europe' and they went their separate ways.

Ken Taylor had said they would have to have me find a way to ship them to Europe. Loren didn't think that quite agreed with his vision but didn't say anything. When Ken got back to his office in Chicago and said he was going to give the Bibles to a Chaplain named Jim Ammerman in Frankfurt. His Editor and Chief, Dr. Wendell Hawley, said, "Kenneth, Jim Ammerman was my supervising Chaplain in Vietnam. When things were so bad in the fall of 1987 at Hill 815 and we had 1300 casualties in ten days time, Jim came up and stayed with me. He prayed with me and encouraged me. Ken, if he needs the Bibles, we will not only give them, we will pay for shipping them." They called me and said the Bibles would be shipped free of charge.

By the time they arrived, my first Commanding General had retired and been replaced by a new General. When his name was announced my heart leaped within me. The name was William R. Desobry, my fine friend from Ft. Hood, Texas. He had just had his third star pinned on. He was with us when those big army trucks bringing the Bibles from the port at Bremerhaven, Germany. The first Bible out of the box was presented to General William R. Desobry. He said he expected that convoy of Bibles to change his command and change what was going on in US Army Europe. Bless God. That is exactly what happened.

The military thinks they know how to orchestrate their forces, they know how to call for air strikes and artillery, Naval weaponry and tanks and helicopters and gun ships but I want you to know that Almighty

God knows how to orchestrate His forces. God was just doing that in providing the Bibles.

Shortly after arriving at V Corps, we were helping Youth With A Mission prepare for the 1972 Munich, world Olympics. Youth With a Mission had just purchased Hurlach Castle, just south of Augsburg, Germany to use as a base for their outreach to the Olympics. Some three thousand people were housed there, trained and prepared to commute daily by train into the Olympic area to witness to young people from all over the world, These were the best athletes that any nation could produce.

The Deputy Chief of Staff at V Corps was my every day working boss. General Harold Aaron had an unusually strong mind. He would be described as a micro-manager. He had a computer for a mind and had twenty-two Colonels working directly for him. If we approached him, he would name the five or six key projects that any one of the Colonels had at any given time. He would say, "Give me an update" on anyone of those he was interested in. He retired as a three-star General. He was a fine man to work for but he demanded excellence in everything that was done.

I asked him if he would accompany me on a flight by helicopter from Frankfurt to visit the Hurloch Castle that he might meet some of the leaders of the YWAM organization. He had become quite interested in what was being done in spiritual things. He was a God-fearing man, but like many Christians, not really aware of how much power and presence of God could be made known in the world here and now.

We arrived at a unit near the castle, were met with sedans and taken to the castle. Many things were going on as they prepared for that great outreach to the Olympics.

I had said to the leadership at the castle, "You simply recognize the General, take us on a tour of the work and share with us what God is doing and what He is putting together with many people from many nations to witness to the others from the world. Don't worry about the General, just talk to us as though he really wasn't there. Don't let it hinder the witness of the gospel."

They needed very much the help of a commercial artist to get some publicity out. They had no contacts so they began to pray. A commercial artist in London, England, was praying about what he should do with his life and God said, "Go to Hurlach, south of Augsburg, Germany and serve Me there with Youth With A Mission.

He flew to Augsburg, caught a train to Hurlach and said, "God sent me, I don't have any talents as a Bible scholar. I am just a commercial artist."

They said, "Praise God. Our prayers are answered." Here was the need supplied for their work.

General Aaron heard many stories like that from the work at the castle before we returned by sedan to catch our helicopter for the flight back to Frankfurt. He looked at me and said, "You people pray. I have always prayed but you seem to get your answers from God when you pray."

"Yes, we try to move under the anointing of the Holy Spirit. General Aaron, do you remember a few months ago when my name was given for the Senior Chaplain of V Corps." He said he did.

The first time he was approached he said, "No, I don't want him." I told him about the all night prayer meeting we had at Grafenwohr when I thought I was coming to Frankfurt and I didn't want to leave Graf. God had spoken a chapter and verse from Ephesians 3:20. "Now unto him who is able to do exceedingly abundantly above all that you ask or think" When I read that, I knew God was going to bless the ministry if I would go and serve in V Corps.

But, you had said that day that you would not accept me, even though you had never heard of me nor met me. I said then, "The prayer meeting is over, let's go to bed."

We went to bed wondering what would happen the next day. Well, in mid morning the next day when the senior Chaplain had gone to talk to you about me, when he walked in the office, you said, "The only Chaplain I want is Jim Ammerman" You see, God does hear and answer prayer."

When I told the story to General Aaron, he looked at me and said, "Is that what happened?" From that time forward, General Aaron never gave me any instructions. He simply asked what I was doing and what I needed to carry out the projects for the Lord.

✝ 21 ✝

HOLY GHOST FILLED CHAPLAINS

Each year there was a Chaplains retreat in beautiful Bertchesgaden. It was the place Hitler used for his retreats. The US Military had the General Walker Hotel, which was located on the mountain overlooking the town. From there you could see the "Eagles Nest" on up to the top of the mountain which was built as a gift to Hitler.

Half of the chaplains would go for one week, with the other half coming the following week. It was on temporary duty orders with our room and board paid for us while we were there. We could take our wives. and have a great week .

I had been there the previous years. I went to my Commander, General Desobry, and said, "The practice is, each Chaplain will be there for one week but I believe that I need to be there both weeks so I can see all of my Chaplains. I will go on orders one week and take leave for the second week if that is permissible with you."

He said, "No you won't. You will be there on temporary orders as your duty station for both weeks. You can come back to the office when the two weeks are over. If that is on your heart it is of God and that's where you should be."

We went to Bertchesgaden and stayed both weeks. God had spoken to me in October that during the two weeks in February, "I want you to minister spiritually to the other Chaplains." I was not in charge of the Chaplains Training Conference. Someone from Heidelburg was. I don't break into someone else's meeting. Besides that, God had said, "I want you to minister to Chaplains and get them Spirit filled." I don't know if you have ever wasted prayer time by saying, 'Well Lord, do you really know what you have told me, do you really understand who you have told me to minister to? Many of these Chaplains did not believe in the Holy Spirit. Some weren't even born again. God would really lean on me. I would be driving down the autobahn in my car and the Spirit of the Lord would come on me so heavy because I hadn't said, "Yes" to the Lord, that I would weep and have to pull off to the side and stop. It is illegal to stop beside the autobahn in Germany unless there is an emergency or you are at a pull off rest stop, but I would be weeping so hard I couldn't get to a rest stop. I would get to where I could see again and go on. I realized God was serious. I finally said, "I will do what you have told me but I don't think the Chaplains are going to like it too much." Now that is a lot of faith. What God has to do in spite of our unbelief!

I called the Retreat Center, knowing the Chief of Chaplains was coming from America, and he would have the largest suite there. The Senior Chaplain over all of Europe would have the second largest suite, I called and told them I wanted to reserve the third largest suite. I thought after the meetings are over at night we will invite the Chaplains to come to that three room suite and it would be big enough to hold those who wanted to come. I had the announcement made at the start of the evening service. I remember the man who was making the announcements. I had it written on a three by five card, and can you believe, a college educated, seminary trained man, would read the announcement as he did. I had written, "Those who want to come to a Charismatic prayer meeting, come to suite # 320 after everything else is finished tonight." I didn't want to interfere with the scheduled program. He gave the announcement this way, "Those who want to attend a <u>cosmetic</u> service...........Chaplain Ammerman will be leading that <u>cosmetic</u> prayer service." Since my name was mentioned, people knew what it would be.

As we rode the elevator up to my room for the meeting, I thought, it really was a <u>cosmetic</u> service. When God gets through with you, you will look better than you ever did before. The spiritual change inside begins to show with a glow on the outside.

We got to our room and the Chaplains kept coming in so that there was no more room. Some were actually on our bed as there wasn't room to stand on the floor. We didn't have a very long prayer meeting that night as they were too pressed in to be comfortable. We read a scripture or two and prayed for the power of God to come down and bless the Chaplains.

Our suite had a door that joined another single room. Along in the night I heard three Chaplains in there kneeling by their bed by the door. They were crying out to God. Many of them didn't get to bed all night as the Spirit of God was on them and kept them awake. God intended to bless. He hadn't thought that up that night. He had been planning this in heaven at least since October, and it was now February.

One of the Chaplains found out there was a big basement lounge in the hotel next door, that would hold about a hundred and fifty to two hundred people. It wasn't being used so he spoke for it. We announced that night that the 'cosmetic' service would be in the Hotel McNair, next door. There must have been a hundred Chaplains there.

As I started to have an opening prayer, one of the Chaplains stood up and said, "Don't do anything until you pray for me." He had his military health records in his hand. He said, "I have three things that will kill me. Someone told me about last night and I got them to release me from the hospital. I have to have a healing or I am going to die." We set him in a chair in the middle of our big circle. His kidneys were failing, his liver was dying and I believe it was his heart as the third thing. They told him if he left the hospital he had to carry his records as he would be in another hospital before he could get back to them. God came over him and the next day he was out on the ski slopes. He was healed and has gone on with a career and has become a Full Colonel in the Chaplaincy instead of dying as a Captain. That was the way the prayer meeting started.

Seated by me was John, a Baptist Chaplain who had served near me. He stood up and said, "Now I want everybody to know I don't believe in this Spirit filled stuff. I don't believe in these Divine healing things, and I certainly don't believe in speaking in tongues. I only came to this meeting because I respect Jim Ammerman," and he sat down. He said that with vigor and conviction.

On the other side of the room was another Chaplain named John. He was an Assemblies of God Chaplain and he stood up and said, "I want to tell you something John, I believe in the things you don't believe in. I believe in the things Jim believes in. I want to tell you about speaking in tongues. I can prove to you out of the Bible, if you don't speak in tongues, you can't go to heaven." He stuck his chin out as he said it very adamantly and set down.

I looked up to heaven and said in my heart, "God, this is what I was saying last fall. This is not going to be easy. Here are these people that believe so differently and you have ask me to bless them spiritually. If you don't come and bless them, the whole thing will turn into a curse.

Help me!" God fell on that place. Every night that week we were up most of the night as God wouldn't leave us alone.

The week end came and the first group of Chaplains left. I knew that another group would be there on Monday. In fact they started coming in on Sunday afternoon. They had heard the Lord was moving and they had come early to get blessed.

On Saturday, I knew I had to get out and get some exercise. I had hardly had a moments break all that week. I took my skies and went to the slopes. I went up the highest Mountain there and skied down part way. There wasn't but a couple others up there yet. I skied out on a ridge, where I could see for miles. It was a beautiful day. I may have seen all the way to Switzerland. I was enjoying so much being there alone and getting away from all of the intensity of the spiritual ministry I had during the week. There on a Saturday morning as I looked, I said, "Oh God, how great You are. This is the work of Your hands. This is Your creation and You are letting me see one of the most beautiful sights, draped in white by the snow that You have caused to fall on these Bavarian Alps." I was just praising the Lord and glorifying His name for the great God we have and how marvelous He is. finally I stopped to catch my breath and was standing there on my skies with that beautiful scene before me.

A voice spoke so loud and clear, I am surprised everyone on the mountain didn't hear. It said something to me that shocked me. I could not believe what I heard. It said, "I will make you the head of the Chaplaincy." I stood there thinking about that. I knew that in the summer, the Chief of Chaplains was retiring. I knew the Deputy would also be retiring, so both the One and Two Star Generals would be replaced by Colonels. In my spirit I knew that was not what God had said. He had not said, "I am going to make you the Chief of Chaplains." He had said, "I will make you the head of the Chaplaincy. It was such an awesome experience I couldn't ski. I made my way down the mountain, put my skies in my van and went back to the hotel. My wife wanted to know why I wasn't out skiing. I told her that God had said something so awesome that I couldn't ski. I had never wanted to be a General. If He had wanted me to, He would have put that desire in my heart but I didn't know what He did want. We hid that in our hearts and didn't tell anyone.

When Spring came and we returned to America, one of those Three Star Generals went to Washington and campaigned for me to become Chief as well as some other Generals who were friends of mine kept in touch each day with the board that was meeting. They called and said, "You are going to be Chief of Chaplains. They are down to three people and you are one of them."

I said to that dear brother, "Please don't say anything to make that happen. God has not given me the desire so he must have other plans for me and I don't want to be out of the will of God." They picked someone else. He was jumped from Colonel and was a Two Star General that night. I was glad it was not me but I still did not know what God had said to me. (This has now happened with the formation of the 'Chaplaincy of Full Gospel Churches,' which I head up).

The second week had began there in Bertchesgaden and one Chaplain came to me and said, "We have to pray now. I have a brother in America who is dying. He has such intense pain that they can't stop. They x-rayed his head and there is no tumor and yet something is just racking his entire body with pain." We got alone over in a little alcove and hardly started praying when God said, "I will show you what is the matter." I saw a man on a construction sight. A large back hoe, a powerful piece of equipment, came up out of a ditch and knocked his hard hat off and knocked him down into the ditch. The vision was over.

I turned to the chaplain and said, "Stop praying for a minute. Has your brother been a construction worker?"

"Yes, he works with heavy equipment doing sight preparation for construction." I asked if a back hoe ever hit him in the back of the head and he said, "Oh yes, a year or two ago. It knocked him in the ditch and he was unable to work for a few days."

I told them the back of his head or his spine has been injured. That is the cause of his trouble. Let's pray and then you call the hospital and tell them what to look for. We prayed and thanked the Lord, and he placed the call. The next morning they called and said, "Yes, we can operate and relieve the pressure on his brain stem and he will be all right."

That is the way the second week started. It was an awesome week and by the end of those two weeks, twenty four Active Duty Army Chaplains, had been filled with the Holy Spirit. Some had to be saved first but it didn't matter to God as He was in the business of changing things.

The Religious Book Store for all of US Army Europe had a display of books for sale in the hall of the hotel. I was looking at one of the books on praise, the first being 'From Prison to Praise'. The author, Chaplain Merlin Carothers, had been in all sorts of trouble but having received a pardon from President Truman it meant he had never committed the crime. This made him eligible to become a Chaplain. He went to school and met the qualifications. God used him to teach that if you praise the Lord, circumstances will change in your life. The end of the book table had a stack of Merlin's books. The Assemblies of God Chaplain, named John, was standing there reading one of them. The Baptist, John, came by. He had been with Merlin at a post when Merlin had gone through a divorce. He did not feel that anyone who was divorced should be allowed to stay in the ministry. Of course the Assemblies John had grown up under the same teaching and here he was reading a book that ministered to him. The Baptist John said, "I wouldn't read anything written by an adulterer. The Assemblies John said, "Have you read any of the Psalms lately?" I had to go outside to laugh. Folks, God knows how to forgive sin. If God would let King David continue on being king after he repented in Psalms 51, for having committed adultery, stole a man's wife and then had the man murdered, I think God really can forgive sin.

There is another thing that happened at that retreat. There were two couples who were missionaries who were doing fabulous work for the Lord. For years they would go through the check points and go behind the Iron Curtain to minister and carry contraband Bibles. They could have gone to prison for it but they believed that the same God that could make blind eyes see, could make seeing eyes blind, so the Word of God could be taken in to people who needed copies of the Bible. They again and again had made those trips for twenty years.

The man from England had a beautiful tenor voice that we loved to have sing at our chapels. He had been slated to sing two songs one evening. After the first song, everyone thrilled at the beauty of his voice. It was a song with a message but before singing the second song he said, "I'm not here to preach or give a testimony but I want to tell you something that happened in England one time when I was singing this song after having sung in churches for eight years, God said to me, 'You sing about Me, but you don't know Me." I realized what God said was true. I was singing and suppose to be a Christian but I had not received Jesus into my heart and life and known Him personally. It may be that some of you, as Chaplains, have been working for the Lord and you know about the Lord but you do not personally know the Lord. You do not have Him living in your heart and soul. If that is the case, while I sing this song, will you just invite Jesus to come in and be your Savior."

Some of the Chaplains got up and walked out into the hall. Being one of the senior Chaplains there, I slipped out and went around where they were. They were gnashing their teeth on the singer. "Who does he think he is that he could tell us that maybe we don't know God. We are the leaders." My heart was heavy and broken with it but we went back and finished the services. After it was all over we went back to the basement room in the other hotel for our prayer meeting.

One of the Chaplains, (let's call him Bob) was under such conviction he didn't know what to do. He couldn't understand the turmoil he was feeling and being so jittery. He went to his room and drew the big deep German bath tub full of hot water. He thought if he soaked in the hot water and had a few drinks he would settle down. He poured himself a glass of whiskey and got into the tub. It didn't seem to have any effect so he drank more whiskey. He told me later that by that time he knew he was a serious alcoholic. Every time he had a service he talked about a God that he did not know so he would have to get drunk to calm his nerves. He kept adding more hot water until it was steaming and nothing helped. He thought, 'Oh God, what is going to happen to me?' He remembered seeing a Gideon Bible in the bed side drawer so he got out of the tub and went after it. He never studied the Bible or prayed a prayer that wasn't in the prayer book. He used only sermons that were published. Here he was sitting in a tub of hot water drinking straight whiskey reading the Bible. He said he didn't know what or where he read but the thought occurred to him, maybe he should try to pray. He said, "I laid the Bible over by the whiskey glass on the little table. I bowed my head and said, 'God, I am in serious trouble. I don't know what it is I need but what ever it is, I want you to do it for me and give it to me.' " He said the presence of God came over him and he started talking in a strange language he didn't understand. He thought, 'Oh, God, I have lost my mind.' He had been afraid he would loose his mind because of being an alcoholic. Every time he tried to pray, it wasn't in English.

He got up and got dressed, put his clothes in his suit case, got in his car and drove straight home. They missed him and he wasn't in his room. They checked the desk and he hadn't even signed out.

When we got home on Saturday, I had a message to call Bob. He was not one of my Chaplains but was in the edge of our area and assigned to a different part of the Army. I called and he said, "I have to see you, something has happened I can't talk to anyone about it but you" I was so tired after the heavy two weeks and the drive of six or seven hours home. I asked if I could wait until the next day as I was to speak at a chapel not too far from him. When services were over I would come straight to his home.

When I arrived the next day he told me what had happened to him in the hotel room and he was at a loss as to what it all meant. When he got home he needed so much to talk to someone, he got hold of a hippie type young man who had tried to share the Lord with him. The hippie told him what he should do the next day. He said, "The way things have been going at the chapel, we need to liven it up. We need to have a Jesus march around the chapel. I'll teach you some scripture songs, we will have all of the congregation follow us and we will march three times around the chapel. We will claim that building for the Lord and then God will be free to move in that chapel."

He said, "I didn't know what to do but this man probably knows more about God than I do as a Chaplain. I play a guitar and I practiced on the song he gave me. I put on my liturgical robes and told the people what we were going to do. We practiced the song a couple of times and then started the march." The only people who went to his services were the very spiritually cold ones or those who went to Happy Hour and drank with him."

"As we went around the first corner outside, I looked back and there were only two of us in that Jesus March. Me and the young hippie." This young man had been saved out of the drug scene and the life style that goes with it, but he still hadn't changed his dress even though he had learned to take a bath and wash his head. Bob continued, "We made our three trips around the chapel anyway but since there was no one else there we didn't take an offering but I did have a benediction before I came over to wait for you. Can you help me understand what is going on?"

I said, "Brother, I can do more than that for you." I took my Bible and began to read to him what had happened to him and what God intended to happen to all of His people.

He was amazed and said, "Oh, this is so good." We spent the whole afternoon in the Word of God, praising the Lord at times and at times stopping to pray. Standing up and lifting our hands thanking God because He had come down in such mighty power upon that man.

His wife was in the kitchen and would look in on us every few minutes. What I didn't know at the time, he normally came home from services and beat her up regularly on Sunday afternoon. He was so frustrated in preaching about a God he didn't know. She couldn't understand what was happening that she had not had her Sunday abuse.

I want you to know that man is retired from the Chaplaincy now and he is the pastor of an Independent Spirit Filled church. God has never turned him loose from that day until now.

✝ 22 ✝

FORT LEAVENWORTH, KANSAS

On the Monday after Christmas, 1973, I received a call from my good friend, the Chief of Chaplains, Gerhart W Hyatt. Will said to me, "Jim, what do you want for an assignment when you return to the States in July of 1974?"

I said, "Will, I know you well enough to know you have my records in front of you as you ring my phone in Frankfurt, Germany, from the Pentagon. I know that in my records, you have looked at my 'Dream sheet' preference for my next assignment which has not changed since December, 1966 when I became a Lt. Colonel. I want to be assigned at the Command and General Staff College at Ft. Leavenworth, Kansas. I want to be a pastor to those young officers." About a thousand successful young, Junior executive level officer from the Army with a few from the other services are moved with their families for ten months each year. They depart in early summer to be replaced by a thousand more.

He said, "Yes, I have that paper in front of me. It has been there a long time." I told him it hadn't changed. I didn't care if I was the number two or number one person but now that I had been promoted, I would be number one. He said, "I can't assign you there, you are too Pentecostal. Well, no..."

I said, "Wait a minute, yes, I am Pentecostal but I don't think that would hurt those fine young officers and their families." He told me he would call back later. He called each Monday morning through the Monday after Easter. The conversation was almost identical. He said, "If I don't assign you there, where do you want to be?"

I said, "I have no second choice. You assign me where ever I am needed and I will go without comment." On the Monday after Easter my phone rang and it was the Chief again. He wanted to know if my desires were the same. I assured him they were and he said he would put his executive officer on the line and I was free to ask for anyone to be moved out of there and almost without exception, anyone to be moved in there to form my team for ministry. I had never been given such a blank check on personnel with whom I would be serving and working.

I told the Executive Officer to leave everyone in place but I would need a senior priest to fill the slot of the one who was leaving. I named the one I wanted, Chaplain Conrad Loftus. Conrad had asked me before he left Europe if I would request his assignment to work directly with me when the opportunity came. I knew he was a born again, Spirit filled priest who loved his people and had a pastors heart. God had already propositioned everyone else I needed for the team at Leavenworth.

I want to share with you some of the things that happened at that historic old post that has had so much to do with the US Army.

I arrived at Ft. Leavenworth and went in to pay my official call on the Commanding General, Jack Cushman. He was a brilliant but demanding man. That is how he became a three star general. Everyone told me, "He is a micro manager. He will grill you with questions." God has given me favor wherever I have been so I wasn't worried. When I reported in he motioned for me to take a chair and we just visited for maybe fifteen minutes. I realized it was time to go and as I got up, he stood up and walked to the outer office with me and said, "I'm glad you are here Chaplain."

When I returned to my office, the phone was ringing. It was the Generals Aide. He said, "I thought you need to know. After you left, the General said, 'Any time that Chaplain wants to see me or call me, he has priority on my time." I hung up the phone and wondered, 'what happened there?' God had given me favor in his sight.

We arrived at Ft. Leavenworth during a hot draught, the first of August, 1974. Our furniture had been shipped from Germany, well in advance of our coming and we thought we would have it in a matter of days, but that didn't happen. First, it was tied up in a dock strike in Houston, It was loaded on a truck and headed for Kansas but the truck over turned and broke the over seas shipping containers loose. It arrived in Kansas City and left on the dock over night, the night the draught broke!

My wife called and told me the furniture had been delivered and they were pouring water out of it. I had better get home. Needless to say, there was a lot of damage and work but through all of that, came to really know God was in us being there.

God had brought two line officers there as students who had stayed on as faculty members, George Kuykendall, a Protestant and Ron Maxson, a Catholic. They had the same vision that I did. They believed we needed to lead people to the Lord, we needed to disciple them. As officers in the military to continue to witness for the Lord, wherever they were sent.

I felt the vehicle to use for the program was an organization called Officers Christian Fellowship. I had become acquainted with it in the early fifties and I knew they were Bible believing Christians. They had a world wide network in the military so there would be scarcely a place they could be assigned without having a contact to be cared for. George and Ron had the same vision.

They already had OCF on the post and had four or five or maybe even six small groups that had Bible study and prayer. I felt there should be a minimum of two dozen. The fact is, we had from thirty to forty groups each year.

George was so blessed over what was happening, he retired there and continues to work with them until this present day of over twenty years. Dr. George Kuykendahl, a layman, is a faithful servant of the Lord and will have more stars in his crown than most ministers.

An interesting side of Leavenworth, a tremendously pleasant place, people refer back to it in years to come as 'their Leavenworth year.' It is an exciting, hard working studious year. There is a Federal Judge that use to be a popular after dinner speaker in the area. He would speak about the haunted houses at Ft. Leavenworth. He would conclude his speech by saying, "Well, let's all go to the bar now and have some spirits we can know and enjoy."

We found many of the houses there did have spirits in them, and we would call them, as the Judge did, 'haunted houses.' We also knew that God is greater than they were. We cleansed house after house. There was one set of quarters for senior officers who had not been lived in for three years. People would move in and have to move back out. We prayed through it and with the authority we have through Jesus Christ, who told us to cast out demons, we got rid of those tormenting spirits.

One set of quarters, known as The Eisenhower House, where he lived as a young major, especially had active spirits which we had trouble getting cleared out as well as many others.

I'm not sure how or why the spirits go to a particular place but I have some theories. There is a big National Cemetery on that post as well as another one across town at the big Veterans Administration Hospital at Leavenworth. The first Federal Prison is a half mile away. The US Army first military prison is there. Many of the most wicked people in the United States have been brought there for over a hundred years.

There had been a German prisoner of war camp. Nine German prisoners thought two others had given away some of Germany's secrets so they killed the two. The others were executed. There is a German cemetery behind the prison. There is one cemetery for the prisoners who died or were executed there. I don't think we know too much about the spirit world, good or evil. I have come to understand that when a person dies who had demons who bothered him, those demons are still in the locale.

Demons have personalities. Jesus told his disciples in Matthew nine, some are worse than others. "This **kind** comes not out but by prayer and fasting." The disciples had waited until Jesus came down from the mountain because they could not cleanse the boy.

Jesus had told a story about a man whose demon had left his house which he cleaned and swept out but he didn't get it filled with God and the Holy Spirit, so that demon returned and found his former place was empty so he brought in seven other demons **worse** than himself, so we have come to learn that demons have personalities. We have learned this in our own experience in deliverance ministry.

There were demons of every sort around Leavenworth. Many were brought in for burial and others have stayed on when the possessed died. This post was established when the Oregon Trail and the Santa Fe Trail left from there. One of the Post Commanders had answered a knock at his door at number one Scott Place, a beautiful set of quarters, and someone shot him dead in his door way. They got on a horse and rode off and it was never found who murdered the Commander. All of these things are a part of Leavenworth History.

While we were still moving into our quarters, strange things began to happen. Items would be moved from floor to floor. Counting basement, it was a four story duplex with twenty rooms. It was a left and right hand copy. In night or day time there would be spirits moving around in our set of quarters.

Some spirits are poltergeists. This is a German name for noisy spirits. One of these spirits made the sound of a woman walking in high heeled shoes. We could hear that on the wooden floors.

There was one my wife would hear in the mornings. After she had cleaned up from breakfast and the family was gone she would sit down in the living room and study the Bible. One spirit we called, 'the log roller', it was as though he would roll a log across the floor of our bedroom above her. We took some of the most spiritual leaders we had and would pray through the house and it would stay free for a period of time.

One night, our daughter, Crystal, was out for the evening and a friend called and left a message for her. Crystal always parked her car behind the house, entered the ground level basement and went up the back stairs to her third floor bed room. We were on second floor. We had retired for the evening and heard footsteps coming up the back stairs, past our floor and on to third. They crossed over our bedroom and went to her room. My wife said she would go give Crystal the message. Only—Crystal wasn't there. Her car wasn't in the alley. She didn't come home for another hour

Our son, Mark and his wife, Sherry, who pastored a church not too far from us, had stayed up late to watch a movie on television and we had gone to bed. After they had retired, which was well after midnight, they heard a woman coming up the stairs in her high heeled shoes, walked some twenty feet down the hall and stopped in the hall, just through the wall from the head of their bed. It stayed awhile and then walked on. The next morning at breakfast they related what had happened and then said, "We now believe what you have been telling us. We knew you believed it before but we thought you were mistaken.

Years later after I retired I came by the post and stopped to see some friends who were still there with the chapel; it was October thirty first. I was shown the local town newspaper and in the center of the page was their Halloween story. Headlines read, "Former Post Chaplain Drives Ghosts Out of Quarters at Ft. Leavenworth." They told the story quite accurate. It had happened many times.

I had read in the paper one morning that at St. Mary's College, Sister Dorothy Hensheid, had just returned from a years prayer retreat in Wyoming. My spirit bore me witness that if she went there to seriously pray for a year in that deserted place, that God had probably done something special with her.

Later in the day I went to the College and introduced myself to the Mother Superior. Mother Superior said, "You made a courtesy call on the Arch Bishop when you arrived and he told us to do anything we could to help you with your ministry."

I asked to see Sister Dorothy Hensheid. When I asked her what had happened during her year's prayer retreat, I already knew what the answer would be. I could see it on her face. She said, "Oh, I got filled with the Holy Spirit."

I told her my request that she consider coming and teaching on the post in the Protestant Sunday School class. I wanted her to teach a Catholic booklet titled, 'Life in the Spirit' which is a ten week class. It begins with John 3:16 and ends with the Day of Pentecost.

She got it approved and we set the date. We had already ordered the books but so many people came, we hadn't ordered enough. We advertised it in both Catholic and Protestant papers as well as the post paper. We had to have the Protestant Sunday School class, taught by a Catholic nun in the Post Theater. At the end of ten weeks, in one hour, over ninety adults were filled with the Spirit. I would say that wasn't a bad ten weeks work. The average pastor in America, doesn't see that many filled with the Spirit in a year. The anointing was on her. God does bless us in working together with any Christians that we can.

All three of the New Years Eves that we were assigned at Ft. Leavenworth, we had a joint Protestant/Catholic evening. We would begin with the Catholic Mass. The priest would give the homily and then he would serve the communion. It is not customary in most Catholic churches but he stated, I never ask who comes to the communion rail to receive the elements of the Lord. He would save some of the elements until midnight when we served both Protestant and Catholic communion.

We would have a 'Progressive Dinner' from house to house. Some would have salads, the next the main courses followed by the desserts. Finally, it would be almost eleven o'clock and we would go to the beautiful little Memorial Chapel, overlooking the Missouri River. We would have a service which would conclude at midnight, with myself and the priest, serving at the communion rail, those who wanted to receive. Some couples, a Catholic and a Protestant, had never received communion together. I would serve one and Father Conrad Loftus would serve the other. There was a release of tensions and a blessing of the Lord that came through those three New Years Eve services. God did many, many things.

One day as I was leaving the chapel a bit after duty hours, an officer came jogging up to see me. He said, "I'm glad you are here. Something has just happened to me I don't think I can tell anyone else about, not even my wife." I took him back, unlocked my office and said, "Tell me about it."

He sat down and got his breath back from jogging and said, "I was over in the Classified Library studying our potential and that of the nations behind the Iron Curtain. I am a logistician and I was doing a study on our strengths and their strengths, our weaknesses and their weaknesses and I realized that in almost every category, they had us outnumbered and it would be a bad scene if we got in a war. I became discouraged and upset about it. I decided I would work my frustrations off by going for a ten mile run."

"I changed into my jogging clothes and took out toward the back of the post to a road that wasn't traveled much. While I was running I was praying." That isn't a bad thing to do when phones aren't ringing and nothing else is in your way to talk to the Lord. He said to God that we were in a bad shape if we get into another war. We are not prepared to fight another war on a World War Three category level.

He prayed, "If we really called on you, God, could you help us, protect us and deliver our nation?" That was the question in his heart and mind that he lifted up to the Lord. Then he said, "Here is what happened. There in front of me as I was jogging, was an angel in the air facing me but moving along in front of me. He must have been fifteen feet tall and had a drawn sword in his hand."

I said, "Dennis, what did you do?"

He said, "I ran right off the road, but I got hold of myself and got back on the road. The angel was there for some period of time. I continued to jog toward him but he stayed ahead of me, facing me. Then he just disappeared. I came right here, hoping I could see you."

This man did know the Lord. He and his wife were very faithful in Bible study and prayer and church attendance but he had not been taught that God is alive and real and well and has miracles on the earth today. This was a giant step that God can do such things today.

With his military mind he said, "But I have two questions. How many men is one angel equal too?"

I tried to run scriptures through my mind for a factual answer and said, "Dennis, I don't know, but one came down one night and killed a hundred and sixty thousand soldiers."

He said, "Oh, that's dynamic but my other question is, 'How many angels are there?' "

Again my mind raced through the scriptures and I answered, "Well, I don't know that either but there are legions of angels, there are ten thousand times ten thousand plus thousands of thousands. However many that is."

He thought a minute and I could see his military mind computing and spinning around between his ears. Finally he said, "Well, if we call on God, and God helped us, there would be no problem would there?"

I said, "That's right brother." We are still in touch with Dennis, who retired as a Colonel and then went to seminary so he could be a better helper in the church with his pastor. He is a business man in California today. He and his wife are blessed of the Lord because he knows the Lord is alive and well in the earth today.

One of the students in the Command and General Staff College always sat with his wife in about the second row in front of the pulpit in that big chapel. He sat there very proper and seemed to give attention but his wife often sat there and would weep. She might cry off and on through the whole service. I tried to catch them as they left but if I would go to one exit, they would go out the other. I found out who she was and I telephoned her at her quarters. I said, "This is getting to me, I have trouble when someone, week after week, through the service is so burdened. Do you need some ministry or help?"

She said, "Oh, I am weeping for my husband. He only goes to chapel to be seen and it looks like he is a very proper, moral Christian officer. He has always been promoted ahead of his peer groups and he wants to do anything that might help his career. Then we go home for Sunday dinner and all he does is criticize your sermons. I sit there by him and it breaks my heart."

I said, "Let's quit crying, let's go to praying. Let's don't pray in desperation, let's pray in faith. I will agree with you before the Lord, that your husband is going to be saved this year. That he is going to leave here as a real Christian and a Godly man."

She said, "Oh, but you don't know my husband."

I said, "That's right. I don't know your husband, but I do know my God. Now will you agree with me that God will do whatever it takes to save him this year?"

One morning shortly after that this lady called me. She said, "Oh, you will never guess what happened. This morning I was in the kitchen cooking breakfast and he was in the bathroom shaving. I heard him call out in fear. I ran to the bath room and he had stepped out into the hall. He was partially shaved, with lather over the rest of his face and the part of his face that was shaved was almost as white as the lathered section. He was trembling. I asked what was wrong and he said, "You remember what I told you? I told you I wouldn't believe in a God like that chaplain preaches about unless I saw God's hand myself. While I was shaving just now, I saw another hand come and wrap it's self around my hand as I was pulling that razor down from my cheek. It was the hand of God!"

Here was a man that had been decorated for bravery in hostel fire, but when God's hand showed up, he was stricken through with a Godly fear. She said, "God is starting to answer our prayers. He knows now there is a God and He is the kind of God you and I believe in."

The follow on to that story is, he got serious in the Word of God, went into one of our Bible studies, was saved and filled with the Holy Spirit. He was transferred at the end of the school year. He went to Europe and was assigned with a British Command Headquarters for a four star General. He held a Bible study and the Anglican Priests, who were chaplains there in the British headquarters, attended his Bible study to learn more about this God who does mighty things on Earth today.

I had a call from a young Captain's wife who was in tears as she called the secretary and asked if the Chaplain was in. My secretary told her I was and I had a little time free before my next appointment. She was in my office in a few minutes. She said, "I have so many problems, and our marriage is about to break up. I just found out why we never have as much money as it seemed like we should for our family. He has been moving another woman around as we are transferred and keeping her. He has her here in Leavenworth now. Don't give me any 'God talk', You just help me with the problems in my life."

I stretched my arms out and crossed them at the wrist. I said, "Young lady, you have just tied my hands. If I can't do any 'God talk' I can't help you."

She said, "Well I don't want any 'God talk' but I do want help in my marriage." I tried to comfort her a bit. That was the best I could do but I said, "On Sunday your husband may be home with you and your two sons and you should be there but maybe you ought to come to our ladies mid-week Bible study and start getting some spiritual food and nourishment so God can begin to do something with you." She didn't say if she would or not but she began to attend.

A couple of weeks later the secretary said she had just had a call and it sounded like the same lady that came in here so hastily. She simply said, "Is the Chaplain here?" and hung up. Sure enough it was the same lady.

When she came in she was so excited I asked, "Ann, what happened?"

She said, "Oh something has just happened that I'm not sure what to think about it. I was watching the 700 Club and they interviewed a man who gave his testimony whose name was Graham Kerr." Graham is also known as, 'The Galloping Gourmet' because of his cooking on television. With his delightful British accent and pleasant ways plus his knowledge of cooking, he had fascinated people. At that time he was the highest paid man in the food industry. She had heard him tell how bad their lives had been and how God had turned him and his wife around. She said, "You know, if God can help a couple like that, maybe he could help a couple like me and my husband."

I said, "Ann, are you ready for some of that 'God talk' today?" She thought she was. She had been a church member since she was young but had not known what it was to know a living Savior and to know a powerful God who could change things and keep you on the straight and narrow for Him.

We talked about the Lord a little then and said, "Yes, the same God who had changed Graham Kerr and his wife Trina, could change you, your life and your home." She went on her way and a few days after that she came dashing into the office and said, "Oh something has just happened that I have to tell you about." She was so excited she could hardly sit down. She said, "This morning I was upstairs making the beds. My husband was at the Command and General Staff College and my two sons were at school. I was so hurting and so lonesome and so disturbed over what is going on with my husband and his girl friend that I sat down on the bed." Ann was a petite little lady, and she added, "I was sitting there with my arms wrapped around my legs, in so much agony and pain. I was trying to pray and I said, 'Oh, God! Don't you care about me? You have helped and blessed other people. I am hurting so much. Don't you care about me?' I sensed someone had entered the room. I looked up thinking my husband had come home and I didn't want him to catch me there in such distress. It wasn't my husband. It was an angel." She stopped and looked at me to see if I was going to believe her. I told her that yes, I could believe it. She went on, "That angel just held me until my heart quit hurting so bad and then he left. I jumped up and came over to see you. I'm ready for any God talk you have for me." Her heart was open to receive every good thing from the Lord.

The last time we saw her in Washington DC, her sons were grown and she was running a Christian counseling center. Her husband still had not let God touch his life but God had truly blessed that young lady and she was a Godly, faithful mother to the children that the Lord had given her.

I have mentioned the women's Bible studies we had on Wednesdays and Thursdays. We had two a week, trying to keep the size of the groups to no more than fifty in each one so we could make it more personal and we could minister to the needs. God worked in so many ways in those women. Some were healed, some set free of habits and addictions.

One woman had back surgery and was crippled for life and couldn't walk. They brought her in and God healed her on the spot. Her husband, who was not a Christian was at church with her the next Sunday. There in the chapel, between the first and second service, I saw her in the entrance with her husband. I went over and introduced myself and told him we were glad to have him there at church with us. He said, "How could I not be here when this is the very building that my crippled wife was healed in?"

☦ 23 ☦

A DANGEROUS PRAYER

The new classes arrived in the end of July, got settled in and were ready for classes which lasted ten full months. September came and I received a call from a lady who said, "My husband is an Army Major here in the new class. I am teaching school. Would you see someone at noon time or after school hours?" I told her I was available twenty four hours a day. She was there at noon time and said, "My husband is not a Christian and I want you to agree with me in prayer that he will get saved this year."

I came around from my desk and knelt down beside her chair. She said, "Now this is the way I want us to pray and I want us together to agree in prayer, because if two or more agree, we can have the blessings of heaven. I want to pray like this, 'God whatever it takes, save my husband before school is out next June.' "

I looked up at her and said, "You know, that could be a dangerous prayer."

She said, "I don't care what it takes, I want Don to be a Christian." I told her that God already had heard the cry of her heart.

I took her by the hand and there with me on my knees we prayed. When we were finished she stood up and said she had to get back to school as she was just there on her lunch break. When I sat back behind my desk, I knew God would do whatever it took to have her husband saved that year.

After the Christmas/New Years break, I received a call from the Colonel who was the Company Commander for all of the thousand students. He told me I may need to be in touch with a certain family as charges had just been brought and we are going to have to have a General Court Martial for one of the students. It was Don.

I tried to call their house but there was no answer. About that time the secretary said there was a couple there to see me. They walked through the door and it was Don and his wife. I asked them to come in and I told them I had been trying to reach them by phone.

They were seated and started relating a terrible story but on their faces were smiles. Finally I said, "Stop, wait a minute. I don't understand what is going on. You are telling me charges have been brought against you from your last post and you are going to be court marshaled. It is one of these cases that is very hard to prove you are innocent, even if you are. You may go to prison and yet you are sitting there with a smile. Please explain this to me. I am getting mixed signals.

She spoke up and said, "I'll tell you what happened. We got this word yesterday afternoon when we returned from our holiday vacation and we stayed up all night and Don got saved. Our prayers are answered."

I hugged both of them and thanked the Lord. Now, I said, "We will start praying about this court martial." That thing dragged on for weeks and weeks and finally ended one week before graduation. In the mean while the Commandant had pulled him out of class as he said to Don, "You need full time to defend yourself. And further more when you are found guilty, it won't matter if you graduate or not."

I went to the General and said, "Sir, you and I are good friends but I want to tell you something. If this man is acquitted, I expect you to do whatever it takes to graduate him along with his class mates."

He said, "I have seen the legal brief on it and he is guilty."

I told him, "Sir, you are the convening authority. You must not say he is guilty. If Congress heard you say that, they would probably force you into early retirement. I respect you too much to have any bad thing happen. Please don't say what you think about his innocence or guilt to anyone else. I will keep that as a perfect confidence but we will have to let the court decide if he is guilty or innocent."

I read through that man's records from the time he was a private as an enlisted man. I called posts where he had been assigned and I knew people. I needed to know how to pray and council them as their pastor. In the mean time they were growing spiritually while they were going through the darkest moments of their lives. Finally the time came for the wind down of the trial. I had been called as a character witness. I told how he had been born again and how his life had changed. I said I wasn't at the other post where the allegations had happened but I believed in him. There was much prayer and some of the ones who brought the charges, fell apart on the stand and began to cry and said, "It didn't happen."

Finally, in spite of all of the mixed signals that had come to the court, the jury was out. I was with his wife and I knew they had two guards there to take him down the street about a half mile, if he was declared guilty, and lock him up in the US Disciplinary Barracks at Ft. Leavenworth. I got a seat directly behind her when the court reconvened for the verdict to be announced. I wanted to be there if she passed out if he was declared guilty.

They called on the president of the court and it was so quiet you could have heard a pin drop. He stood up and said, "We find Don, not guilty." We had people praying at the chapel while it was going on and we sent someone over to give them the word. There was such rejoicing in that court room that they really could not dismiss. The Court dismissed it's self in praising the Lord because there were several Christians there who had been praying.

This wife, who had said, "Do what ever it takes, God, but save my husband this year." had her prayer answered ten days before graduation but it had taken five and a half months of anguish for it to happen. They had met the Lord, and left there really, really, knowing the Lord. God does know how to hear and answer prayer.

Shortly after that, maybe six or eight months later, the top General in the entire US Army, called the Army Chief of Staff, was paying us an official visit. I knew he was a long time friend of General Cushman. I received a call from the Generals Aide wanting to know if I could meet the General and Chief of Staff over at the Memorial Chapel which was about three minutes away from the Main Chapel where my offices were.

The Memorial Chapel was a beautiful stone building located on the hill overlooking the Missouri River. It was built about the year of 1878. We used it for weddings, funerals and some of the smaller services .It was from here General Custer left on his fateful trip to Little Big Horn Montana and there are many memorabilia on the walls of the rich history it holds.

I went there to meet General Cushman. When he introduced me to the Chief, he said, "This is Chaplain Jim Ammerman, my installation Chaplain, but he is more than that. I consider him a member of my faculty because he is teaching Army Officers about God. I just wanted you to know him." What he had in mind was, he was wanting me to be made Chief of Chaplains but he didn't tell me that in front of the Chief of Staff. We visited a bit, I thanked them for their time and returned to my office.

No one was in the office when I went in, and I closed the door to be alone. God had called something to my memory. This was the Fall of 1976. Thirty eight years before, in 1938, God had come over me and I had gone to my secret place in the dense woods near our house. The Spirit of the Lord came upon me and I heard the words only when I spoke from my mouth. It didn't come through my mind. God had said, "I will use you to teach Army Officers about me." Being a farm boy in Southern Missouri, I had never seen a service man in uniform at that time. I went to the library and checked out a book about the army but I couldn't understand what it meant about officers, non commissioned officers and enlisted so I had dismissed it.

I sat there as I wept on my green uniform until I had dark blotches from my tears. You see, I had forgotten that word from the Lord. In fact, three years later, I had so forgotten it, I did not join the Army for World War II, I joined the Navy. God never forgets what He says. God brought it to pass anyway and carried out His plan and purpose for my life.

I sat there very humbly in that chair, thinking, "Here I am, I had been a full Colonel for some time now and realized that God had ful-filled His plan in spite of me. From the lips of my Commanding General, I heard the words that reminded me of what God had said. I indeed had done what God had spoken. When God speaks a word, I don't care if is for thirty eight years, a year, a day or the rest of your life ahead, it is history when God speaks it. It will come to pass.

✟ 24 ✟

So Long Army—Hello World!

In my office at the Fort Leavenworth Main Post Chapel while I was alone for a few minutes, the phone was not ringing and no one was scheduled to come in, I sat at my desk praying. While I was praying and rejoicing in the goodness of God and the wonderful things that were happening by His Spirit's move, I stopped and the Lord spoke to me. He said, "The time has come. Now get out of the Army." It was so clear and certain, that I stopped everything, even thinking, to make sure what I had heard. When I fully realized what I had heard, I called my wife and said I would be home for lunch. I normally did not go home but would have a working lunch with some of the staff. I went home and told her what God had said. We had enjoyed the Army, it had been a good life and it was a big decision to leave. I wondered what my wife would say.

Her reply was, "I am not surprised. I'm ready." She had been planning to refill the deep freeze with a supply of meat and other items. She would put things in the basket and then put it back where it came from in the freezer. Somehow she knew she was not to fill the deep freeze again. We entertained many people and normally kept much food on hand. God cares about us even down to having the deep freeze emptied in preparation for a move away from the Army.

We began to look at the calendar to discern when God wanted us to leave. I began to think in the natural and thought we would retire in the early summer when the class was complete in the Army College. As we prayed about it the Lord told us to "get ready now." I was obligated to give the Army at least a ninety day advance notice for my retirement. I did that and we retired on one March, 1977.

We prayed about what we should do upon retirement. We had no plans made whatsoever. We began to receive calls from various places around the world. One was from the world wide ministry we had used so much in Germany, Youth With A Mission. The leader, Loren

Cunningham, asked if we could minister in twenty two nations around the globe at his training camps, schools or workers in various places. We got out the world atlas and began to plan our trip, heading West. We taught first in Hawaii and then on out through the Pacific, Australia, Asia, Europe and then back home.

We planned on when we should return. Every trip should have a terminal point. We had already heard about the meeting that was coming up in August in 1977 in Arrow Head Stadium, on the east side of Kansas City, Missouri. It was the first North American Renewal Conference on the Holy Spirit. It was an international meeting of Spirit filled people. We very much wanted to be there to be blessed by that great gathering.

AROUND THE WORLD

We started out on our trip that lasted for five months and one day. God blessed us every mile driven and every mile flown, over forty thousand miles. We were back in time for the great conference in Arrow Head Stadium.

Some of the experiences on that trip were beautiful illustrations of the blessings of God. One of the first places we stopped was in American Samoa. Among other things besides teaching at their camp they asked for me to go with them for their weekly prison outreach. There in that mandated island, under the United States Government, they only have one prison. It doesn't matter if someone is in there for thirty days for a speeding fine or for three life sentences, they are all in together. It is a very poor arrangement.

At the appointed time we went there and met the Captain but the man who was supposed to play the piano and lead the singing in the Samoan language, did not show up. The Captain on guard said, "Well, I didn't want you in here anyway so you can't go in if you don't have music."

I asked the YWAM leader if there was any way we could get someone else to play and sing for us. The prisoners all understand English but it is not their native language. Whether you have thought about it or not, you can praise the Lord and read the Bible better in your own native language, rather than a second language, even though you use it for a life time. There is something about our native mother tongue that is very precious to the heart of a man or woman. They said there was a woman who lives near by who can play and sing. When she came the Captain of the Guard said, "No woman can go in this prison." We had somewhat of a discussion about it and I explained who I was, I was just a traveling missionary and I understood prison work. I have had military prisons under me. After a while he finally agreed we could have a service but from the time he let us in, we were to be out in exactly one hour. That doesn't leave a lot of time to minister to prisoners with songs, scripture, message and altar call but we accepted his terms as that is the only way he was going to let us in.

We went into the prison and every prisoners there came to the meeting. One of the reasons they came was, one of the few ways that people in Samoa get off of that island is by joining the US Military. They heard I was an Army Colonel and they wanted to come meet me as maybe I could help them get in the military and escape that little island. I didn't realize that until after the service was over. I had wondered why each and every prisoner wanted to attend the service. God has His way of getting things done.

We didn't have a very long song service as I planned more music at the close when we invite people to come to the altar. There we were, people seated in what was the center of the prison with cells all the way around three sides and offices down the fourth side of the prison. Guards were at every corner and some watching from the office windows since all of the prisoners were there in one compound together. As I began to speak I felt a tenseness instead of the anointing I wanted to feel. I thought 'what is resisting the move of God?' I only spoke a few minutes after reading some scripture and I stopped as I felt so much resistance. I silently prayed, 'Oh God. You arranged for us to have this service, what is it You want done?'"

The Lord spoke and said, "There is a prisoner here who has tried to pray and he has felt that never once in his life did I hear his prayer. He feels spiritually destitute." I repeated to the men what God had said.

A man rose to his feet and said, "I am that man." As he stood up, the men almost held their breath. It was absolute silence. One of those silences you say you can hear a pin drop. I didn't understand that and had to have it explained to me later. At that time I said to the man, "Would you come up here because tonight God is going to hear your prayer.

God does not stop a service for one man and tell the condition of his life, and then send that man away empty. I know my God too well for that."

The man came up there and everything was silent. The guards were all standing at attention, some with their weapons drawn. I found out this man was in there for three life sentences. He was the meanest man there. The prisoners were all afraid of him as he would assault them if he didn't get his way. The guards were even afraid of him. He had spent much time in solitary confinement on different occasions.

As he came forward, I ask everyone to please bow their heads and pray for this man. They wanted something to happen to him as they didn't want him to be as mean as he had been. I put my hand on the top of his head, still not knowing who this man was but knowing he was not just an average prisoner. As I put my hand on his head and began to pray, the power of God fell and I felt the heat of the Holy Spirit go through my hand. This tough, hardened criminal, began to weep out loud. He said, "God has heard me. God has heard me. I know that God has heard me this night." We prayed for his soul's salvation, out loud, in front of all of these people. Then it was that he said, "Let me tell you who I am and God has done a miracle in touching me tonight."

At that point, the Captain of the Guard came over and said, "You can stay here as long as you want to stay. If you want to stay all night, we will keep them right here and have services all night." The guards were so happy that the worst problem they had in the prison had suddenly been changed and would be a part of the answer instead of part of the problem. I asked those who wanted to be prayed for to stand up. Every man in that prison stood to their feet. I am glad the Captain let us have a lot of time because the five of us who came for that service, prayed for people on into the night. God changed that prison by touching the heart of the worst prisoner there, at the start of the service.

I think God did hear his prior, previous prayers but that was the night that God would not only save his soul but many others because he was touched by the Lord when he knew for sure that God had heard his prayer.

We went on to New Zealand, a beautiful country, with wonderful people. Anyone who gets to go there is certainly blessed. Among the highlights of our time in Auckland, New Zealand was when I was holding a one day retreat for sixty to eighty ministers at a retreat center in the hills outside of Auckland.

Shortly before lunch time, a man drove up in an expensive car, wearing a very expensive suit. I assumed he was not a pastor but he simply introduced himself as Bill Sabritsky, thinking everyone knew him, but Jim Ammerman didn't know him. He said, "I have made arrangements for late this afternoon to pick you up and take you to my home for the evening." and he left. I asked who he was and was just told he was Bill Sabritsky. Others were there and I didn't get to ask who Bill Sabritsky was but I noticed that before five o'clock he came in and sat down in the back. I could tell people held him in esteem, making sure they spoke to him and he had the way to move around in the group of men. Finally he said, "Come get in my car." My wife had stayed the day with our hosts, a medical doctor and his wife, so it was only Bill and I.

As we got in his car which was a beautiful Rolls Royce, for little throw out rugs to keep the dirt from the floor of the Rolls, he had white lamb skins. As I got in I felt like I should take my shoes off.

I told him I had a problem, somehow the Chinese Embassy hadn't taken care of our visa for there and neither did the Australian Embassy get them back. We turned them in and I am afraid I won't get them back. We are suppose to fly out day after tomorrow, and tomorrow we are scheduled to be outside the city.

He said, "I'll take care of that." He got on his mobile phone. Remember, this is 1977 and mobile phones weren't plentiful anywhere in the world and certainly not in New Zealand. He made one call and said, "We can stop in front of the Embassies and they will bring them out to the curb to us. I told them we would be there in a few minutes and they are to have them ready."

I was quite sure then that this was not some preacher with a Rolls Royce, white lamb skin rugs and that kind of influence. He still hadn't told me who he was as he assumed I knew.

We arrived at his home which covered well over an acre. He showed me a little suite of rooms in which I could rest. I asked just what was going on tonight. He said, "Every Thursday night I have a lot of people gather in and we just have a prayer and ministry time in my home. I had been a church member for years but I got saved on a Thursday night so I consider that a special night of the week. Unless I am gone overseas I have the meeting. You just rest a while and pray so you will be ready to help me tonight. We will call you on the intercom when it is time. We always have a buffet meal every week for those that travel some distances for the meeting. We will call you in time to eat. I have already made arrangements to have your wife brought to the meeting.

When he paged me, the house was so large, I got lost and had to get on the intercom and ask someone to come bring me to the meeting. When I got to the main room for the meeting, even the padded folded chairs were color coordinated. It was so lovely it looked like 'House Beautiful' in America. It would seat ninety people in the main room but it looked to me like more than that were showing up. I asked him how all of the people were going to get in this room. He said, "Oh they can't, I have other dens, libraries etc. I have closed circuit TV from where we will be into these other rooms. When they see on the TV that people have been ministered to in the first ninety, and have left, they will see the empty seats and begin to come in from the other rooms and will keep the ninety seats full until everyone has had ministry. We won't dismiss until they have all been ministered to.

I found out later Mr. Sabritsky was a lawyer, a real estate developer and one of the wealthiest men in New Zealand who probably had the largest yacht going in and out of Auckland Harbor.

Before he was saved he blew the horn on his yacht and expected everyone to get out of his way. When he drove, he expected the highway to be free in front of him. Now God had saved him and given him a ministry.

A few years later Mr. Sabritsky was asked if he would travel the world with Derek Prince. Derek is noted around the world with a terrific, miraculous anointing on his ministry. Derek said, "Mr. Sabritsky is more anointed than I and I wish he would travel the world with me." He has been in America and other places.

We were privileged to be in that mansion that night and watch God do many miraculous things. The main thing I learned that night, which I needed to learn and have used ever since in my ministry. It is now twenty years later and I still need this bit of knowledge I learned in Mr. Sabritsky's home.

Some of the people we prayed for would fall in the floor, as though under the power of the Holy Spirit. The first time this happened that night, the woman had come forward and given her prayer request. Bill said, "Let's listen to the Spirit a minute and see what He says your greatest need is." This man would hear God so clearly that he would say, "Yes we will pray for your crippled leg, but that's not your big need which is ...."

To one lady he said, "Yes we will pray for your son's broken back but your big need is the affair you are having with another man, not your husband."

God spoke through him in an awesome way. The first one that went down, 'under the power of God,' was a fake, only I didn't know that. The devil will pull people down to stop them from being ministered to. The people ministering will think God has touched them and go on. That person will go home as bad off, or even worse off than when they came.

A psychiatric nurse came and said, "My need is ...."He prayed for her, she went down and he lifted her right back onto her feet. He said, "Don't play opossum on me. Satan, you leave her alone. We are going to minister to her and you are not going to pull her down on the floor." He turned to me and said, "See, that wasn't God. That was the devil." It had never occurred to me the devil might do such a thing. I had not been practicing discernment .Then he said, "Now we are going to minister to her main need. She works in a psychiatric hospital and God says many of those patients have demon's and some of those demons have fixed themselves to her. Now we are going to cast those demons out and the power of God will deliver her and she will be free from that and also healed for the reason she came to this altar." I stood by that man for some four or five hours and ministered along side of him. What a privilege. I have carried that learning in my ministry around the world ever since.

One lady became so excited over a vision she had she could hardly wait until there was a break in ministry to share it. In the vision she had seen me, to put it in her words, "preaching and ministering in the funniest church building." She described the building in detail. She was a member of "The Church of England" and normally went to church in a grand old cathedral.

She described a building that was made for live theater performances. She described in great detail how part of the platform extended out into the congregation. There were lights around the stage top which was curved up from the sides with a dip in the middle. It had a black back wall to the stage. "It was the funniest church."

I recognized the place and told her I was scheduled to be speaking there for a three day Holy Spirit conference when our tour was over. This was where The Beverly Hills Baptist Church in Dallas, Texas held their Sunday services. We thought it most unusual that the Lord would show her where we were going to be. What could be the purpose?

About a month after the ladies report of the vision, my wife and I were flying from Bangkok to Chang Mi in the north of Thailand. We were flying up a valley between two high mountains in a twin engine turbo prop plane. The clouds covered the tops of the mountains. After we started, we hit a terrible turbulence. The pilot said if we went above the clouds we couldn't get back down and there was not room enough to turn around between the mountains. He had to proceed to Chang Mi. The weather was so bad the two hostesses were buckled down and even they were sick. The silverware and dishes were being thrown around from the bottom to the tops of the cabinets. Everything that was loose was flying around in the cabin of the plane.

I was seated in the aisle seat with my wife by the window. She sometimes gets a queasy stomach and I looked over at her wondering what her reaction would be. She was sitting there relaxed with a smile on her face. I said, "Aren't you worried?'

She said, "Oh, no. I know we are going to be all right. Don't you remember the ladies vision back in Auckland? We are to be in that church in August. Nothing is going to happen. God is taking care of us so why should we worry about this storm?

God cares enough about us to even spare us needless fear. He saw that storm months ahead and sent us peace.

On two separate occasions while we were overseas, once in the mid east and once in Hawaii, my wife, who is a good wife and mother, heard a word from the Lord concerning our youngest son, Steven.

On one occasion as she was awakened in the night, we found out later it was the very hour back where Steve was in the United States, she was very fearful and disturbed that our son's life was in danger. He had spun out on a motorcycle on a turn in some gravel and rolled over and over, peeling skin off of him. In all logic, he should have been killed, or at least had a broken neck or back, ——but GOD! She awakened me with a great sense of urgency and said, "Let us pray. Something grave has happened to Steve." We prayed, instead of being seriously injured, he only had superficial cuts, abrasions and contusions. He was able to go about his normal duty although in surface pain.

On another occasion a half a world away she again woke me. That time he was doing assembly on high microwave towers, as much as 600 to 1400 feet in the air. He was near the top when a man working above him dropped a tool. Our son did not have his hard hat on and was struck on the head. He fell toward the ground but one arm caught in a V of the structural steel. He was hanging there unconscious. The other workers got to him and strapped him to the steel but he came to and insisted he was all right. They unstrapped him but he passed out and fell the second time. This time his heavy tool belt around his waist caught on the way down in one of the angles and held him. This time they strapped him to themselves and worked their way down with him.

We firmly believe that our prayers, though a half a world away, caused God to send an angel to appear on the scene and save our son's life. God is a great God and He cares about us day or night, whether we are in the same area or somewhere else. God is powerful and supernatural all the time in our lives.

We had arrived in Afghanistan early in the morning. To this day it is dangerous to let it be known where you are located if you are a servant of the Lord. Christians are not welcome in that land.

At the airport I told the man who was directing the taxis that I wanted a taxi cab driver who spoke English. They motioned to one, he came over and I said, "Do you speak English?" He replied with the only word he knew in English, "Yes." We didn't know that was the extent of his vocabulary until we were well across town. Only a few of the main streets in Kabul, Afghanistan have names. The lesser streets are not named at all nor do they have house numbers.

The only information we had was given to us by a missionary's wife who remembered what little her husband had told her, from the one time he had visited that mission house in Kabul. That's not much. I had made a few notes about how possibly to get there. I was told it was not too far from the Russian Embassy and was closer yet to the Sieman's Corporation of Germany, that had a plant in Kabul.

We arrived in the center of town and were proceeding on past. I tried to communicate with the driver, and found he understood nothing. I tried to get him to take us back to the airport. He didn't understand, or didn't want too. Finally we came to a five - way intersection and I persuaded him to stop the taxi.

I said, "We are going to set right here in this cab until we hear from God. We are going to ask Him to direct us across this sizable city. At every corner, He must direct us whether to turn left, right or straight ahead until we find the mission house.

Before we started that five month trip, we had prayed an awesome prayer. We didn't realize how awesome it would be. We had said, "God, as we travel around in ministry, we want You to sensitize us to Your Holy Spirit, so we will hear the softest whisper and feel the gentlest nudge of Your Holy Spirit guiding us."

Now we were in a strange city, in a strange land, unable to speak the language, without a map and not knowing how to find the mission house. God was answering our prayer, but it was a very strenuous, tension filled moment for us. As we sat there, the sun began to warm up. We had to roll the cab windows down. The cabby was wondering why we didn't want to proceed on and would turn and motion if he should go ahead. Some people would come and look inside the cab at these foreigners.

The women would peek through the slots of their facial coverings. If a woman has eye contact with a man it is considered a sexual invitation. My wife wore sun glasses and kept her eyes down and wore long sleeved blouses and stayed very close to me for the time we were there.

Finally, I said to the cabby, "Russian Embassy," His face was blank. I tried several things and finally used the German word "Ruskie." His face brightened up and he said, "Ruskie, Ruskie." He started the cab and drove furiously a mile or two to the Russian Embassy. Of course this wasn't where we wanted to be, we just knew it was near by. When he drove up the gate was open and an armed guard was on either side of it. He didn't stop at the gate, he roared right on in, right up to the Embassy door. I thought we might get shot. They called ahead on their walkie-talkie radios and four guards came running out with weapons drawn.

I told my wife, "Stay in the car, do not move." In that part of the world were a lot of car bombs and suicide drivers. They were alert to being blown up. It was a very tense moment. The driver got out and could communicate with the guards a little bit. The guards looked in at us and we sat perfectly still. Finally the driver got back in the car and we drove outside the Embassy and stopped.

At this point, the poor driver was totally confused, I said, "Now let's drive ahead." When we came to a corner I would motion for him to stop while I prayed, "God, which way do we go?" We moved a block at a time for two or three miles across that city. Finally, within my spirit I heard God say, "This is the block." I had the cab stop on a dirt road in a residential area. I told my wife, "Stay here in the cab. Our suitcases are in the trunk." I got out of the cab; in my heart I knew it was to the right. I walked to the right one half block, going slowly. I wondered how I would know when I got there. All houses had high solid walls around the yards, with broken glass and barbed wire on top of the solid gates. About the middle of the block I heard the voice of a young English lady calling the dog. She had only arrived the night before and was unfamiliar with the country. The missionaries had left her there alone for the day, with the instructions of "DO NOT open the big gate to the fence, let NO ONE in and keep this big German police dog with you." The dog needed to go outside and she had let the dog out. As I came by, she was calling him back to her. Isn't it amazing she called just as I was there!! God is awesome.

I called to her and she was afraid to answer. I could see through the crack in the fence that she was going back into the house. I said, "Please, Young Lady, would you come and just look through the crack in the fence at me. I had the name of the missionaries but they were different from the ones she had met. I said, "If you will just look, you can see my wife at the cab. We are an American couple coming to the mission house."

Finally she said, "I'll tell you what I will do. I will unlock the swinging gate that is a part of the large gate. You wait until I get in the house or I will sic the dog on you. Then you can come in the yard and wait until the missionaries return." I motioned to my wife, she got out of the cab and we went inside the compound and sat on the porch until the missionaries returned, because she was afraid to let us in due to the dangerous situation in that country.

We had a letter of introduction but they had not received our letter telling of our visit. In such an austere society there was much ministry needed for the hurting people. Even though we were caring for their physical needs, we knew if it was found out we were witnessing to those people in the Name of Jesus, that we would be placed in jail and probably executed the next morning. If not that, given what would amount to a death sentence, being placed in one of their jails. Their food and especially their water, is so poisonous to people who are not use to it that to be sent to jail would no doubt bring our death. God directed us across a strange city, with no map, corner by corner and let a young lady call a dog at the right moment. It was one of the most astounding, tension-filled days of our entire life and yet, God, as always, was found faithful.

✝ 25 ✝

PASTORING IN DALLAS

During the time I was Pastor of Beverly Hills Baptist Church, in the Beverly Hills section of Dallas, Texas, God was present in many ways. During the first week I was pastor there, as was my custom, I arose early every morning to pray. God clearly said, "I have a six month plan and I have a one year plan for you in this church." I made a note to remind me of it later on.

The church was behind many thousands of dollars on land they had bought for the construction for a new church building. During that first six months. between mid-June and Christmas, all bills were paid and we were financially current on everything. That was a time of rejoicing.

There had been some fantastic blessings of God. As one woman had arrived at church, she had slammed the car door on her daughter's hand and broken her finger. It was a compound fracture and that little ten year old girl had sat through the service with the pain of that hand. Finally after the service was over, we had prayed at the altar and people were leaving, she came up and said, "Pastor, I want you to pray for my daughter." She had her hold her hand out and the broken bone was pushing against the skin.

I am going to confess and be real honest. I looked around for a deacon to see if one could take them to the hospital but they had already departed. I will admit it was not with much faith that I prayed over that little girls hand and they left.

The next Sunday morning while announcements were being made, this mother and daughter came to the platform and asked if she could say a few words.

She took the microphone and said, "Last Sunday, here is what happened......." She told that story but she told it the way it needed to be told. She said, "You know, the pastor didn't pray much of a prayer over my little girl's broken finger. He just sort of prayed a prayer to get rid of me, I think, but before we got home, that finger was healed. The dislocation of that finger was gone. My little girl was healed and I want to give God the glory."

I stood there with my head bowed, realizing that God was good in spite of my lack of faith and unbelief.

The phone rang on Sunday afternoon just before Christmas. A lady said, "Pastor, will you pray? We are at the store and were looking at a bicycle my son wanted. It was on display on a stand and some other children were spinning the wheel. He stuck his finger in the spokes and it cut his finger right off. He is bleeding badly and we are going now to the hospital." I asked if she wanted me to come over but she said, "No, just pray."

They reconnected it and bandaged it. Some two or three weeks later she came to the platform at church and said the finger is dying. X-rays show the bone is shriveling from both ends. Tomorrow they are going to remove his index finger. Will you pray he not loose this very important finger? There before the church, we all prayed.

We got a call on Monday afternoon. She had requested they X-ray the finger again before removing it. Even the bone had grown together. The finger was healed. He had only a slight scar and complete use of his finger.

Blessings like this were happening in that Spirit-filled Baptist church and yet, God released me from it. I thank the Lord He did, in His own way.

On the same day in December, the 15th, that I became pastor in June, I was going over my next day's work and schedule with my secretary when I realized it was six months to the day since I had come there. I was thankfully we were financially in good shape but I somehow felt God meant more than that when he spoke to me six months before. I called it to the secretary's attention that it had been six months.

She said, one of the staff wanted to talk to me. The Youth Pastor came in, visited a bit and said, "With your permission, I would like to submit my resignation."

I told him we would miss him but if he really felt that was what God wanted him to do it must be. I really did love that young man. He is a very successful pastor today. I knew the people loved him and especially the young people. I reminded him the agreement was that we give a months notice. He said he was submitting his notice as of then but he had a months leave accrued and he would like to take it during the month of notice.

This meant he was leaving that very day.

That took me by surprise and I began to wonder how we would get along without him with no notice, especially with Christmas coming up. I saw it was really on his heart to do it that way, I concurred with him.

There were three doors into that office and as he left by one door, the secretary brought another staff member in from her office door. He came in and said virtually the same thing. Here were two principal staff members on exactly the six month day. I commented to the Secretary, "Well, God said he had a six month plan. These are three items on it. I wonder what else is happening that I do not know."

God had said he also had a one year plan. I began to realize there were many people in leadership in that church that really had disqualified themselves in being leaders, if ever they had been qualified. I am not going into the dirt and dregs that is in many churches but this church had not been exempt from it's problems

In the meanwhile, we had a television program and the station manager called saying they needed to talk with us concerning renewing our program contract for the next year. The business manager and I met him for lunch and found out they were tripling the payment for TV time. There was no call for that but the decision had been made by the owner of the stations. He had his own reasons for it which I won't go into but I do not concur with. We said we could not pay that kind of money. It was high enough to begin with.

We began to have meetings to work on the problems that were in the church. My goal has always been to try to restore someone who has gone astray or bring them up to where they should be if they were sub-par in any way. We began to work on this but unfortunately, it wasn't that well received. Due to this, a few months later we had a parting of the ways.

About this same time, the most unusual thing happened that I have ever been aware of in my entire life.

In our master bedroom, we had the head of the bed facing north. The street in front of our house runs east and west, with houses on either side of us.

One night in my sleep I began to dream. Perhaps you have been asleep and dreamed, and yet were aware you were dreaming. That is what happened in the initial period of this dream.

I began to realize that spiritual things were going on in this dream. I remember thinking, not only am I dreaming, but this dream has some spiritual significance to it. I wondered what is causing me to have such a dream.

What was happening was, there were angels and demons fighting. The demons would come up with a lie and it would push the angels back. I could see them over on the east side of the house in the neighbors yard as though there was no wall there and yet I knew I was still in my bedroom.

Then the angels would get together and find the truth of what had been said instead of the lie. They would speak the truth and with that truth they would drive the demons back through the entire length of our house and across the vacant space and into the yard of the neighbors on the west.

The demons would come up with another lie and drive the angels of God back through the house and bedroom where I was and out into the neighbors yard. This happened several times.

Let me tell you, this is how spiritual battles are fought! They are not fought with weapons as we think of war. Spiritual battles are fought with truth and lies. When we get to the truth of the matter we can always defeat the enemy and his lies.

While this was going on, my wife suddenly set up in bed and said, "Jim, there is a big bird in here!" She had been awakened, heard the fluttering sound and vaguely saw something in her peripheral vision cross overhead, in the dimly lit room.

At that point, I realized, I had moved from a dream into a spiritual dream or vision and was setting up in bed, leaning against the headboard of our bed, watching this take place.

It was the early hours of the morning by then but sleep had gone from us. We got up, made a pot of coffee, mused over this, prayed awhile, and wondered what was the meaning of it.

We related this story to a very spiritual couple whom we have known for many years in the military. They thought about it and prayed about it awhile and here is what they said, " We believe that battle was over you and your future. That is why God let you see it." One thing I will always remember is, spiritual battles are won by truth, the devil only wins battles when people accept his lies. I thank God for being very real at a time I needed some strong encouragement in what God was having us do.

I want to explain just a few words as to how that happened. I do not intend to point a finger at anyone.

It was Wednesday night and I had been so busy that day that I did not get home to eat a meal before the mid-week service. I called my wife to meet me at my office.

As I was awake that morning at daylight, praying and reading my Bible, suddenly the burden for that church, for doing anything or for anyone in that church, lifted from me. The feeling I had toward that church, when the burden for it lifted, which had been on me for months and months, was as though I knew there was a church there but it was a matter of history, not a matter of personal involvement. Still, I went to the office that day, met my appointments, did not even take time for a meal. I had a sandwich brought in for lunch. I did it mechanically. More than once that day I said, "God, what is going on that I do not have a burden for the church of which I am pastor?"

When my wife and I walked in the front side door, we saw that the entire building was packed with people. As I looked around I saw people who were members of that church whom I had kept out of jail because they had a wife and children. They had broken the law, yes, but I had gone on their behalf and kept them from being locked up. I saw all who had not been faithful in their attendance.

My wife took her usual seat near the front and I walked up to the platform where I could see better. I said to the fine young man who was our music minister, who still lives in this city, saved and spirit filled out of a Roman Catholic background, I said, "Marcus, you have never before seen what you are going to see tonight." He asked what I meant.

I said, "I want you to lead the music as you always do but this is preacher firing night tonight and I am it. I don't want that to bother you tonight and I don't want it to bother you in the future. You keep your eyes on Jesus. Don't let worldly things disturb your faith."

This was a typical Baptist church preacher hanging. All of the unfaithful members and those who have found disfavor with God, because of their life style, showed up.

With the service ready to start, I pulled a three by five card out of my pocket and walked from the platform to my wife. I handed her the card as I didn't want people to know what I was really doing. I said, "Dear, tonight is preacher hanging night. You are too short to see who all is here. Try not to get disturbed. God has already released me from this. We are going to let this little charade play it's self out and then we are going home."

After it all happened, I came back to her, gave her my arm to escort her out with me. She fainted and fell in the floor. I have never seen my wife so stressed out as she was then. They had persuaded one of the finest people in that building, a pastors widow, to read the motion to fire me. She had believed all of the things they had said. Her son, a pastor here in Dallas, came to me and apologized. He said, "Mother didn't know what she was doing." He wept on my shoulder.

I said, "I know that Brother. Your mother is a fine Godly woman. Some people deceived her, that's all. I harbor no feelings against her whatsoever."

God had released me, I knew it and God knew it. That is all that really mattered.

After our non-scheduled, unexpected, sudden departure from Beverly Hills Baptist Church, we found ourselves back on the road again in ministry. We traveled all of the forty-eight states, Europe and out in the Pacific ministering.

✝ 26 ✝

A New Ministry Formed

We were in Berlin, ministering with General Ralph Haines, who now serves on the board of Chaplaincy Full Gospel Churches. We were invited there by an American Army Retired, Colonel Gene Byrd. He had been the Commandant of Spandau Prison when the people who were convicted in the Nuremberg war crime trials were there.

Part of their sentence was that they had absolutely no communication with anyone except once a year with close friends or relatives. Colonel Byrd felt he just must witness to them about Jesus. This was reported and greatly upset the Russians. America, France, Great Britain and Russia jointly controled that prison. They finally agreed to the Americans that if he would leave the prison and retire immediately, they would not press charges in an international tribunal.

Col. Byrd retired but stayed on in Berlin. He had invited General Haines and myself to come minister to German men. We had one of the most fantastic weeks of ministry that I have ever experienced. Germans will set for two to three hours and listen to dry lectures. You can imagine what they do when something alive and real is going on. The first time I spoke, General Haines had flown in and I had caught the over night military train in. They picked me up and took me straight to the meeting. As he finished his teaching, I was introduced to speak.

Much prayer had gone into this but at the most four or five people in that large room that had ever seen God do miracles. As I stepped up to speak, God said, "I don't want you to speak at all this morning." The interpreter, who was reading my introduction, when he finished, I said to him, "Tell the people I'm not going to speak or teach this morning." He looked at me quizzically and told them. In the meanwhile, I am saying to God, "What am I suppose to do? They brought me here to speak."

God said, "I am going to show My power and glory in this room." I had the interpreter who was head of the Berlitz institute in Berlin, and had only been a Christian a short while, tell the people that. Everyone, including my good friend, General Ralph Haines, and Gene Byrd were looking at me wondering what was going on. There was time while the interpreter was talking to the people, for me to ask God, "What next?"

He showed me a German man sitting over to my right with a wine-red jacket on. God said, "Call him up here. He is suffering from an extended dislocated left shoulder."

I asked him to come up and did he have a shoulder that was dislocated?

He said, "Yes, I do. That's the reason I was sitting near the door, so I could slip out if the pain became unbearable" Germans are known for being stoic. There was no expression on his face that he was in pain when God spoke to me and I looked back there.

I asked, "Would you like to have God heal your shoulder.?" He said he would but did not understand at all what that meant.

While the interpreter was telling him that, God said, "Ask him about his right hip that was hurt in a car wreck twelve years ago."

When I asked him about that, he really got interested and said, "Yes, that's right but how did you know?"

I said, "God is looking at you this morning and I am His servant here in this room."

He said, "But I have learned to live with my broken right hip and I hardly limp anymore."

I told him, "I don't think you are going to have to live with it at all anymore. I think God is going to take care of both it and your shoulder." I reached over and touched him on the forehead and said, "In the name of Jesus, be healed."

He started throwing his arms around like windmills and jumping up and down like a jumping jack. As he did, he was leaping around the platform and letting out kind of a Texas cowboy yell at a rodeo. Everyone was watching this. He got completely around behind me.

I was trying to see what was going on in the minds of the people. I had just then seen a US Army Officer come in. He was a Lt. Colonel, in uniform. He started walking down the aisle, carrying a large camera case with him. My first thought was, he had come to take pictures of General Haines but as he got closer I could see by the insignia on his uniform that he was a doctor. He introduced himself as Colonel Clark Ballard, and "I have never seen anything like I have seen here this morning. I am the senior American psychiatrist in US Forces, Berlin. I deal with cases that takes maybe five years to get any improvement. Here I have seen miracles in front of my eyes. I need this kind of power in my practice."

I asked if he was a Christian. He said he was but he had never seen God do anything like this.

I said, "If you want the anointing of God, you can have it." General Haines had come up by me and asked if I wanted to instruct him about the Baptism of the Holy Spirit or should he?

I said, "Sir, this is a German meeting and the Germans are waiting for us to minister to them." I had told the interpreter that anything we said, to tell the people in German. Germans are very impressed by titles and rank in a structured society.

I said to General Haines, "Let's just lay hands on him and pray, God will fill him with the Holy Spirit and we won't have to instruct him very much." General Haines said he had never done it that way but go ahead.

He was taller than either one of us but we reached up and laid hands on him and he began to walk around the platform speaking in tongues. When he had gone through West Point, he was a champion shot put thrower. He had big biceps that he was flexing up above his head as he went back and forth praising the Lord.

While he did that a line had formed down the center aisle. I asked the interpreter what these people wanted. He answered, "They want what the Colonel got." I am happy to report, they 'got what the doctor got.' They got what the man in the red jacket got. They had a week of the Lord's blessings.

A reporter was there from the largest newspaper in Berlin. The owner and publisher of that newspaper invited us over to his private penthouse offices. He kept a moving sign going on top of the building, insulting the Communists across the wall. He was a loyal, patriotic citizen of Free Germany. He had a special luncheon for the General and me. He said to his people, "Puff those meetings. Let everyone know where these meetings are." So many came we could not get them in. Beginning Monday morning and going on through Friday evening, God worked all week.

At the close of the last meeting we were taken back to where we were staying which was the nicest place the military had because of the four-star General status of General Haines. We were relaxing before going to bed and General Haines said, "I would like to talk to you about something. You know, we don't have our Independent, Spirit-filled Full Gospel people represented in the military chaplaincy.

General Haines had retired as the Vice Chief of Staff. He had been over the Continental Army Command with six hundred thousand troops under him. He had commanded US Army Pacific, during the Vietnam time. He was the number two General in the Army. The only one over him was General Westmoreland, in the Pentagon. He was a very important man and a very good Spirit-filled Episcopalian.

He said, "Jim, we need to get the doors open and have our Independent, Charismatic, Full-Gospel ministers to become Chaplains, and you are the one to do it."

I said, "Yes sir, we need that and I will pray about it."

He said, "Let me tell you, you have been out in the civilian life a few years, you know pastors, you have been on radio and TV nationwide,............" and he gave me all the good reasons why I should be the one. I told him we really would pray about it."

Again he said, "Our Independent Full Gospel people don't have to have a cathedral to worship in, they don't have to have pipe organs, they can take a guitar and strum on it with some scripture songs and preach the gospel of God and help change the US Military. You are the one to do it."

I said, "Sir, when we get back out to Heidelberg, my wife is there, and we will begin to seriously pray about this."

A four star General is use to having the answers given of "Yes Sir" when he expresses his desires. He said, "Well, I think it is time to go to bed. I don't really think you are listening." That is the nearest thing to a cross word that General Haines has ever said to me. He is one of the most gracious men I have ever known. I was serious in what I was telling him and I was listening to him but I knew if there was ever a Full Gospel Chaplaincy, it had to be by the Word of the Lord and that was why we were going to pray.

My wife and I returned to the States and began praying about a Full Gospel Military Chaplaincy. We had a few close friends join us and we prayed for fourteen months. After about a month of praying, most Christians expect an answer from God. We started hearing from our friends, "Well, what if God wants it done this way............what if God wants that done..........?   My wife said we were going to have to hear from the Lord. I said, "Yes, and to do so, we are going to have to leave Dallas, go where no ones knows what we are praying about. Before you got up this morning, the Lord said we should take another missionary trip around the world."

She said, "We can't do that. Remember the basic transportation cost twelve thousand dollars and we don't have it."

I said, "Dear, if the Lord wants us to go there will be money. We can visit missionaries, work with them, fast from time to time, pray daily and no one will know what we are praying about. Then, we will hear and it will be the Lord and not someone trying to help the Lord by telling us what we are to do and how we are to do it;"

She said, "Well, we will just have to wait and see." A day or so later there was a knock at our door. A man we had met in Dallas but had since moved away, was standing at the door. I had never seen him well dressed. I knew he was Spirit-filled but that was about all I knew. I said, "Frank, please come in." He said he would only be a minute, that God had told him to come bring me this check. He handed it to me, folded over, face to face.

When I opened it up, it was a check for six thousand dollars. I said, "Young man, don't give away all of your money. Someday you will want to get married. You need to plan for your future. You need to take this back, you shouldn't give away all your money."

He said, "Pastor, I haven't given away all of my money. My grandfather bought some penny stock years ago." I didn't even know what 'penny stock' meant. It was a term I hadn't heard. He said, "We cashed that in a few days ago. It become worth so much I bought a nice home in the city where I now live and I paid cash for it. I like classical music and I like the best literature. I have all of it in my home. That new Buick there is paid for in cash and I have tithed on the money. God said to bring you this check."

On that basis I said I could accept it. I said, "It is almost lunch time, my wife is cooking. Let me have her come in and you stay for lunch." I headed back to the kitchen to tell her and he drove off without our even being able to thank him.

I jokingly said to my wife, "Well, I have the money for my ticket, where is yours?" I changed it to, "No, we will both go half way."

We sat down with a world atlas and began to plan a trip, going to Europe first, through the mid-East, across the Western Pacific, all the way from the Southwestern part, up to Japan and back home.

We hadn't even told our family what the Lord had laid on our hearts but we planned the trip, knowing the basic cost would be $12,000.00. I want to give you a report on what happened, before the week was over. Remember, we had $6,000.00

A letter came in from a man in Europe, whom I had never met. He said they wanted to have a Holy Spirit Conference in beautiful Bertchesgaden, Germany. They didn't want to get involved in a lot of red tape with the government but, "If you and your wife will come and be here for a week, we will take care of your expenses in country for hotel and meals. When you leave, we will give you a check for $3,000.00. It was for the date we were already planning on being in Europe.

I received a letter from a Chaplain that used to not believe in super natural things for today. He said, "I am a senior Chaplain in Korea now and I want you to come over for two weeks in Korea and minister to our Chaplains about the spiritual things of God, here and now, in this time. I would like for your wife to come to be available for speaking and ministering to the wives also. I will have government money for it. It is a lot of paper work if we get involved in transportation. What I would like to do is write a contract with you. Come and stay two weeks, we will take care of you while you are in Korea and when you leave we will give you a check for $2,000.00. My preferential dates are...................."

By this time we had already figured out a schedule and would you believe, those were the dates we were going to be in Korea!

We then received a letter from Loren Cunningham. Youth With A Mission headquarters had been moved from Switzerland to Hawaii. He said their work had grown so much he needed to have a leaders conference. He wanted me to come teach the leaders and help them get organized for the new level of ministry. He said if we would come either one of two weeks, they would take care of our expenses and give us a check for $1,000.00. We looked at our schedule and we had planned to be in Hawaii one of those two weeks. God had already provided $12,000. We started on that trip.

In Europe we were having breakfast one morning with an Army lawyer and his nurse wife. The lawyer is a man that really hears from

God. I had known him to know when a soldier needed help, even to hear the very name of the soldier, that he had never heard, and tell me so we could minister to that person. Steve excused himself from the breakfast table and came back with a check book. He said, God says He is having you start a new ministry and it is going to take some money to do a feasibility study on it. He wrote out a check for $1,000. I used that money for the initial ground work for starting the Chaplaincy of Full Gospel Churches. God really was in this ministry, so much so that I tell people repeatedly, "Don't give Jim Ammerman any credit for the Chaplaincy. This is a work of God. God has done it and He and He alone, deserves the credit.

✝ 27 ✝

CFGC is Born

We got back from the trip and I received an envelope with no name or address on it. In it was a copy of the public law that has to do with the Military Chaplaincy. There was no explanation. When I read it, I saw something I had never noticed before. It said, (meeting certain conditions,) that, " ministers from denominations and like faith groups" can have their ministers become chaplains.

I scheduled a meeting with the Armed Forces Chaplains Board in Washington, to meet with them about us starting a Full Gospel Chaplaincy. This board is comprised of the Chief of Chaplains of each of the three services, Army, Navy and Air Force which is a two-star General in each case and their Deputy which is a one-star General. That is six Generals and Admirals. Each has a full Colonel sitting behind him to answer questions that they may not have the answers for, which is called the "Personnel Action Group. or PAG Board. They weren't all there but enough there for a quorum.

I explained to them what I was there for and they finally said, "Well, there will never be an Independent Full Gospel Chaplaincy. I asked why and they said because only denominations could have Chaplains. I had made copies of that public law which I passed around to each of them. They read it and looked at me with a strange look on their face because now they knew the law would allow it.

One of the reasons they were determined not to have an additional Chaplaincy as I was proposing, was because the fact that today, though we have 264 military Chaplains under the Full Gospel endorsement, it does not mean that there are 264 more Chaplains in the military. The number is determined each year by the appropriations bill and the personnel rider. The general rule of thumb is, for each 1,000 military persons, there is one Chaplain. The fact we added ours, simply meant that when the Chaplains from the old line denominations would retire, decide to leave the service, or per adventure, God forbid, be killed, one of those spaces would go for one of our Full Gospel types to fill it. They were going to have to give up their places and replace the slots with our Chaplains. Again they said, "No."

I told them that right then I had a man fully qualified. He was young enough, healthy enough, fully qualified as to education, which was four years of college, three years of seminary minimum, plus two or more years in the pastorate." When can I tell him that I can endorse him to become a Chaplain?" Today he is our senior Army Chaplain on Active Duty.

Their reply to me was, "Tell him to go somewhere and find him an endorser. You will never be one."

I stood up, looked each of them in the face and said, "There **will** be a Full Gospel Chaplaincy because God has said there will be and I know He will do what He said. Good day Gentlemen." and I left.

I went to my room to get my things together to return home. I had flown there with an open-end ticket, not knowing how long it might take. I called my wife and told her to meet a certain plane. She asked if we had our confirmation that we had heard from God. I told her we had and she wanted to know what it was. I told her I would tell her when I got to Dallas. I wanted to see her face when I gave her the report. In the natural, all I had heard was, no, no, no and never.

When I got off of the plane I said, "Do you know how we got our confirmation that we heard from God? The world said 'no' and God said 'yes.' The world always says the opposite direction from God so I know we are going to have a Full Gospel Chaplaincy."

What Washington did was make us work thirteen months, digging through red tape. They changed regulations, they changed procedures for administration time and time again. We were almost worn out but during that time God gave us some real encouragement. First of all, no money was coming in and yet we had hired some people to work for us as we had to do paper work as you always have to do to get along with the government. Washington would change the kind of report we were to turn in on how many churches we had, how many members they had, where were they located. First they used the same system the census bureau used and then said, no, that wasn't what they wanted. We had to do more things, ten times over than any denomination ever had to do.

During that time we were trying to find out how many Independent Full Gospel Churches there are. I had no idea. I thought there might be 100,00 church members. We needed to find out so we could get into the Chaplaincy with our proportionate share as time went on. I also wanted to be really spiritually in tune with the Lord. We went to Tulsa to attend the Word Explosion which was meeting in Oral Roberts University's Maby Center.

We were staying in the hotel across the street so we could meet everyone possible among all of those spiritual leaders. As we were finishing lunch one day, Kenneth and Gloria Copeland were being seated near us in the restaurant. At that time we only had one piece of paper describing the vision God had given us. We hadn't printed any literature beyond that. It was one basic paper. I walked over to the Copelands and said, "God has laid it on our hearts to start a Full Gospel Chaplaincy. Here is a paper describing it."

He looked at it and said, "This is God. God has had me thinking about the military Chaplaincy, I'm not qualified, I'm too old but God has been saying, 'Chaplain, Chaplain, Chaplain' to me. I know this is from God. When can I meet you so we can talk about this?"

We met the next morning for breakfast and he wanted to know how he could help me get it started. I told him I didn't know but the first thing that needed to be done was get the word out to as many pastors as I could. He told me to get some literature prepared and he would write a cover letter and send it to 3,000 pastors immediately. That was all done within the next week. God worked like that repeatedly.

During that time, I had some of my best friends of long standing that should have been willing to help financially to keep us going but they didn't think it was possible to accomplish my vision.

We spent from our own resources, everything we had. We had some investments that we cashed in. I sold one of my cars and used the money for trips I needed to make. Our immediately family, sons and daughters gave what they could. Together, we invested a quarter of a million dollars before the Chaplaincy began to support it's self as a ministry.

At one time we were so short on money we had a garage sale and sold things we really didn't want to sell for money to buy groceries. All of our retirement we could possibly spare we used direct in the ministry.

Almost two weeks had gone by after the sale when my wife asked if I had money. I said, "Dear, do not count the money in your purse." I had given her a portion of the sale money and kept a portion. "I realized today, that I have spent more money out of my wallet than I put in it and I still have money in there. I am not going to count it. God is actually multiplying our money to take care of us and feed us while we go ahead and do His work concerning this Chaplaincy."

I'll tell you folks, it is a lot better not to have money, and wonder where it is coming from and let God supply it in a miraculous way than any other way you can get money.

I remember one long time friend, a retired Colonel we had served with four times in the Military. He and his wife had a lot of money and all he did every day was check to see how much his investments were making. I had asked, "Ivan, how long before this thing is going to pay off. How long before we get a Chaplain?"

Using investment terms, he looked at me and said, "Jim, all you are offering people now is 'blue sky.' That means there is no substance to it, there is nothing they can see, there is nothing you can say has been accomplished. All you are talking about is having meetings and praying. No one is going to invest in that kind of 'blue sky.'

We lived with that attitude for over two years until we finally got a chaplain on Active Duty. One time after the thirteen months were up and we had complied with everything the Pentagon had said and they would change it again so they didn't have to do anything with us. I said "I can't stand it. I can't stay in the office." I went outside to trim the lawn. I had a power trimmer but instead of using it, I got a pair of hand clippers and was on my knees trimming the grass along the edge of the sidewalk and praying. I said, "God, we have done everything you told us to. We have done without, we have given up everything we had invested, we have sold our car, we sold an investment house. We prayed and we worked diligently. Yet, the answer from heaven is 'yes' but the Pentagon is 'no'. God, what is going on?"

I stopped what I was doing and I began to weep. When I got hold of myself and was silent there on my knees, (God had me in the right position.) He said, "Trust Me, My son" Just four words.

Now those four words didn't have a lot of definition to them concerning the Military Chaplaincy but I'll tell you, I leapt up and ran back to the others in the office and said, "God has just spoken to us. He said 'trust Me, My son." They could tell I was excited but in a way they were disappointed. I said, "First of all, He spoke to us, and secondly, He called me, 'His son.' That's good enough for me to go on for as long as it takes for the Pentagon to do something."

Would you believe, one week later, we got a letter from the Pentagon that said we could place our first Chaplain. You can, indeed trust God if you are His child.

It took five years before a financial break through came. We had people tell us a new ministry would take three to five years before it would be self-supporting. We thought we were dealing with something that people would catch on to quickly. Besides that, we were not novices. I had been in ministry since 1946 and this was 1984. I thought that would lend some credibility, but money did not come in for a much longer period than we expected.

Both of our daughters married Army Officers. When the oldest daughter's husband retired, they bought a house in the next block from us. Our son-in-law use to come on the first day of every month and give us a check for the ministry. He said he couldn't do what we were doing but he would keep our hedges trimmed, our lawn mowed, our cars cleaned and we were free to give ourselves full time to the Chaplaincy work.

He had been giving these checks quite awhile. I was in Virginia Beach as the 700 Club had invited me to come share about our work. By then we had seven or eight chaplains. It had been raining and I was wet from my rain coat down so I had gone back to my room to get dry clothes. When I opened the door the phone was ringing. It was April 15, 1985. My wife told me that Don, our son-in-law had died of a heart attack. Our daughter was left with two little boys to raise.

While we were ministering to her and helping her work through her grief, she asked us one evening how long Don had been giving a check to help with the ministry. My wife said, "Oh, I don't know, about two years." She said she would really like to know exactly.

My wife thought this a bit of a unusual request but she went to the books to check. She handles the funds and is officially the treasurer of our 501C3 organization. She told Beth it was exactly twenty four months.

Beth said, "You know, that is very interesting. Don had said, "The Lord has told me, I am to support that ministry for two years." We thought churches would be supporting enough by then than we wouldn't be needing to give to it every month. The two years are up but that isn't really what God said." Little did we realize that Don would only live twenty-four more months. Don was faithful and I am sure he's reaping the rewards in heaven these days.

We put the first Chaplain on duty in July, 1984. The door opened. They would give a Chaplain space for about each 100,000 church members the endorser represented. We would be given the slot, we would submit the clergy name and they would become a chaplain. When they realized we were ending up with hundreds of thousand church members, then a million and now seven million, they changed the system. The Navy changed first, followed in a few months by the Army and then the Air Force. They said, "You can submit all the people you want but we will decide who is the best qualified." They have not told us what their criteria is they use for choosing. They really thought Full Gospel people would not be well qualified and they wouldn't have to let them on duty. Maybe a very few.

The fact is, we are giving them the best qualified people they are getting. One Army Chief was retiring and I went to see him to tell him 'good-by.'

He said, "Jim, where are you getting such super qualified people?"

I said, "You know we don't have a system or structure like denominations do. God brings them in touch with us by the direction of the Lord. We do not do any soliciting."

He asked, "How many total people do you have in the Chaplaincy in all three services that have earned Doctorate degrees.?" I didn't know as that isn't a criteria. It is in their records but we do not keep track. I thought maybe six or eight He said, "You have more than that in the Army alone." I knew then they had been checking up on this.

We have consistently until this day, put more Chaplains on duty than the denominational groups have. God has really done it.

The last service to let us have a Chaplain was the Air Force. I made an appointment with the Air Force Chief of Chaplains at Bolling Air Force Base. The Air Force Lawyers and Chaplains have one building that all sides of it are glass. We were meeting in a corner office that had double views and sun light. The General had three of his senior Chaplains in the office with him. They were going to tell me why we couldn't have a single Chaplain in the Air Force.

I said, "Gentlemen, I am going to be fair with you and give you a copy of the letter I have addressed to the Inspector General and to the Equal Opportunity Officer of the Air Force. If I am not given a Chaplain space, I am going to start an investigation. I have been patient now for over five years, waiting on you since we got our first Chaplain in one of the other services. There is no reason for it." They were upset about it of course.

About then a secretary stuck her head in the door and said, "You may not have noticed in this well-lit room with sunshine on both sides but all power just went off on Bolling Air Force Base. There is a fire in Building # 1 by the main gate. They think there are explosives in that building so they have turned off all power and closed the Air Base until an 'all clear' signal is given. No one is suppose to be on the streets until then."

I knew what God had done. He had locked me in that room with those four senior Chaplains. I reached down in my brief case and pulled out a Bible. I said, "There is no one in this room that understands what it means to be Spirit Filled. I would just like to, from the scriptures, explain to you what it is about our people and what God is doing with them." For an hour and a half, I taught them about the things of the Spirit of God. Two were Lutheran, one Episcopalian and one Southern Baptist. Just as I finished with what I thought I should say to them, and closed my Bible, the secretary stuck her head back in the room and said, "It is all clear." It cost them hundreds of thousands of dollars to bring in three suburban fire departments trucks besides the Air Force's equipment but it was in the plan of God.

They said for me to go on home. They would give me a Chaplain. The space opened up and before the week was over we had our first Air Force Chaplain. This has been a work of God, not of any human being.

CHARLENE WRITES

We started Chaplaincy of Full Gospel Churches strictly on faith with no earthly financial backing. We just knew God had directed us to do it. Being responsible for the office, I made the checks out to pay the bills on time but I had to be very careful to not put checks in the mail until there were deposits to cover them. On a good month when the first of the months bills were paid, there might be as much as two hundred to two hundred and fifty dollars left. Never more.

I believe the Lord was testing us to see if we were serious or not. We found it was necessary to sell one car and a piece of investment property to keep the bills paid on time.

One day the secretary came to me and said, "Charlene, I don't understand it. I have gone over this bank account three times. I know I haven't made a mistake. We have $6,242.00." We all praised the Lord.

Three days later, during a heavy rain storm, I discovered water was coming through the vent in the bathroom. The carpet was soaked.

When the rain was over, Jim went up to inspect the roof. In the valley on the south west corner of the house the shingles were cooked off with the bare boards showing. We had to have a roof last month.

We got estimates and guess what it cost? $6,000.00. We still had our $242.00. Isaiah 65:24." It shall come to pass that before they call, I will answer."

God doesn't say he will supply our "greeds" but he certainly will supply out "needs" when we are yielded to Him.

ENGLAND

During the time we were doing all of the preparatory phase and before we had Chaplains that kept us busy visiting them and interviewing those that wanted to be, we continued to minister.

I had been asked by a man in Wales if I would come to minister in Great Britain. My wife and I went for three weeks in 1985. We were scheduled so tightly we could hardly get around.

There was a church in Birmingham, England that had a very unique set up but they didn't tell me what it was. There were two ladies that didn't get to go to the mission field because World War II started. The Lord told them to start a church and He would bring the mission field to them. They had a dynamic, large church, Spirit filled, and they pastored it for their life time. They had a service on Saturday night, Sunday morning and Sunday night.

They did not tell me two things about the church that I would have like to have known but maybe it was just as well that I didn't know.

One was, they had a few dozen pastors from around England that would come to the Saturday evening services. I wondered why the man who had made out our itinerary had not given me a schedule of the appointments that he had made for us. I trusted Malcolm White, a Welshman whom we had known for a number of years, to take care of our schedule.

What really was going on, all of the pastors came in to listen to the speaker on Saturday evening and if they felt he was a man of God and the anointing was on him, they would get with Malcolm and request a time in the next three weeks to be at their church.

The other thing was trickier than that. We had a delightful song service and following the service, they introduced my wife and I and turned the podium over to us. Just as I opened my Bible to read, remember we had just finished a good song service when there was a stirring of God. A man, not native to England, came forward with an 'utterance.' I closed my eyes and carefully listened for God, thinking he was giving a message in tongues and knowing God might give me the interpretation for the congregation. When God didn't speak anything to me in a couple of minutes, I went ahead and read my scripture and completed the service.

They told me later, "You have really passed the test here that we give guest speakers. That man is from Pakistan originally and when he is moved upon by the Spirit of God, he doesn't give a prophecy. He reverts to his own native tongue and prays and glorifies God. We have had people from all over the world try to interpret what he said. No one had gotten close yet." It is good for you that you did not try to interpret the Pakistani language." I thought that amusing but not very nice.

✝ 28 ✝

IN THE EYE OF THE STORM

During Desert Shield, Desert Storm, 1991, Twenty-nine of our Chaplaincy of Full Gospel Churches chaplains of the Army, Navy, Marines and Air Force, served in that war. Others were displaced and taken to Europe to release others to go forward.

We received much help from our Spirit-filled churches and ministries as well as individuals who cared about our military over in the Mid-East, which the Military began at that time to refer to as Southwest Asia.

Many miracles happened there in the Desert. I have one that has been printed from a friend of mine that came to know the Lord and began to be moved by His spirit, while he was at Leavenworth at the Army Command and General Staff College.

This gentleman, at that time was a Marine Major and he did not want to go to an Army school. He really wanted to go to a Marine equivalent school. His father was a Marine, a brother was a Navy officer and he wanted to be with the 'sea-services' which was his choosing from the start. God had other plans for his life and brought him to Ft. Leavenworth, where he found Christ as his Savior.

During Desert Storm, then Major General (2-Star), Krulak, experienced a true miracle of God in providing a well where there had been none, which flowed at the rate of 100,000 gallons of pure water a day for the duration of the war. He calls it "God's Well in the Desert," and gives God the glory for a true miracle.

General Krulak is now four-Star and is Commandant of the entire US Marine Corps! This dedicated Christian Officer is known for his sterling character and his Friday morning Bible/Prayer times with his staff. Thank God for top leaders who know and serve our Lord Jesus along with their country!

In 1995, we had several of our Military Chaplains, some were Reserves, some were Active duty that worked with the boat- people in Guantanamo Bay, who were Spanish from Cuba and also from the Island Nation of Haiti. They were leading them to the Lord by the hundreds and had no literature to give them. The Chaplains were crying for Spanish literature to put into their hands.

We were having dinner with a pastor friend and his wife, Jimmy and Joan Hester who were planning to leave in three days on a missionary trip to Russia. I asked Jimmy if there was anything he was needing for the trip that had not yet been provided. I could tell by the expression on his face that there was so I asked him what it was.

He said, "We promised a Russian General that if he would put us in front of 100,000 Russian troops, to minister to them, that we would bring enough Russian language Bibles to present to them. Jimmy said, "We haven't been able to locate them and even if we did, we don't have sufficient funds to purchase them, even at the price that they sell for in Russia, which is very cheap compared to US prices.

I said, "Well, time is short but let me get on the phone tomorrow and see what we can do." Early the next morning, I started calling.

I knew Terry Law in Tulsa, has many facets to his ministry, but one of the most effective ones is printing the Bible in the language of the people, wherever he goes to work.

I called Terry's office but the secretary told me he was in China, passing out Bibles. Ben, his deputy was there and she put him on the line. Ben was so uptight over something that he didn't even say, "Good morning." Instead he said, "Jim, Terry is away and we have a big problem. We have lost our lease on a warehouse in Moscow and we have to get 110,000 Bibles moved out <u>this week!!</u>

I said, "That's no problem. We have a team, under Jimmy Hester, who will be there within seventy-two hours who will pick them up. Fax me the name and numbers. I will give Hesters the contact and they will take care of it. It will really be a blessing to them.

He said, "I have a second big problem. Terry had it on his heart to print 35,000 Life and Teachings of Jesus, in Spanish to be used for the displaced persons in the Guantanimo Bay area. Now, no civilian shipping can get in there by air or by surface. I guess we just can't get them there."

I said, "Ben, I know the military outfit that has charge of the mission, of controlling the boat people and feeding them. They are keeping them in camps of one thousand so they can doctor them and take care of them. I will call you back within the hour and tell you the contact so Uncle Sam's forces will take those Spanish scriptures into those boat people."

What Ben did not know, was that we had just had a call that there were 30,000 boat people in Guantanimo Bay and there were close to 10,000 that they couldn't handle in Guantanimo Bay and they had been moved into Panama. I called Ben back after calling my Sergeant Major friend who was in charge of the logistics of that operation. I told him he would receive a call from a certain person. They would come to the nearest air base to you, pick them up and before you go to sleep tonight, that literature will be where God wanted them, when He spoke to Terry Law and had him publish them.

God had heard the prayers of our Chaplains for the Spanish literature.

As the 'draw down' began to happen in the Spring of 1991, from the 100 hour war, I was praying early one morning in my home. I had been aware since January there was going to be a serious reduction in our Armed Forces. As soon as the war ended, this began to happen. Plans for it had already began when we were still building up and increasing our Armed Forces for Desert Storm.

As I prayed there alone, I prayed, "God, what will this mean to our work and the Full Gospel Chaplaincy?" Over the years I have learned, that when you pray and ask God a question, you should at least be polite enough to wait and see if He wants to answer you.

I waited. God spoke very clearly to me. He said, "When this draw down of the Military is over, you will have more Chaplains than ever before by actual head count. Since the military will be decreasing, while your Chaplains are increasing, therefore you will have a much larger percentage of the Military Chaplaincy than you have now in 1985. We are writing this book in the Summer of 1997, six years later. I want to report to you that we do have one half more Chaplains than we did in Desert Storm. While the Military has been decreasing well over one-third, we have increased. For the last two years we placed, in Army,

Navy, Air Force, Marines and Coast Guards, and in our State and Federal Prisons, as well as VA Hospitals, more than one Chaplain per week.

God is doing great things. I don't know where all of this is going to take us. It doesn't really matter because, if Jesus is Lord, and the Bible says He is, than you can trust Him to do what should be done in your life and in the work He has given you to do.

✝ 29 ✝

MIRACULOUS MINISTRY AS GOD WANTS IT

Our youngest son-in-law, Ed Leach was selected to teach at West Point Military Academy. We were visiting with them on Easter weekend. A couple who had heard about us through mutual friends came up to us after service and introduced themselves and said they wanted to meet with us.

Then they said, we have a cadet we have been having in our home who is going blind. Will you pray for him?"

We said we would if he wanted to be prayed for. We went to our daughter and son-in-laws home and were eating dinner when the door bell rang. There was this couple with a young cadet in his uniform, standing very much at attention. They came in and said he wanted to be prayed for.

I asked if he was a Christian and he said, he was. I asked if he had heard about people being healed when they were prayed for.

He said, "No, my family nor church ever taught me that."

I read a few scriptures to him and then asked if he was ready now for us to pray for him. He said that he was. The couple said, "Before we pray, let me ask a question. If we pray and he doesn't get healed immediately, should we pray again or not?"

I said, "I believe in praying until you get your answer. I know it is all right to pray three times because Jesus prayed for the same thing three times in the Garden of Gethsemane. So, my word to you is, don't give up praying until victory comes."

I laid my hand on top of his head. This young man's name was David Peters. Others placed their hands on his shoulders or on top of my hand. I didn't pray very long, just a minute or so and I felt the heat and power of the Holy Spirit go through my hand, into this young cadet. At that very instant he began to weep out loud. We stopped praying and waited until he could talk to us. He said, "I felt God touch me." He looked around the room and said, "I believe my eyes are getting better all ready." There are two things I want to say here. I am just as human as you are and I thought, 'is God healing him or is he just trying to see better?'

The other thing I want to relate, before we prayed, I had said, "God may touch you and heal you in one of three ways. He may do it through doctors."

He said, "No, not that way. They have sent me to the best doctors the Army has and they say I have an incurable, un-treatable condition. I will be blind in the next two months. The Army has been so good to me to let me finish this year. The prognosis is, I will have to finish the rest of my education in Braille."

I said, "Well, you have two more chances. He can heal you instantly, in a flash, or He can heal you gradually over the next several minutes, hours or even days." That is when we prayed. David was a very conscientious young man and he asked if he could be taken back to his room to study. The military had been so good to let him stay when they knew before Thanksgiving he was loosing his sight and here it was Easter. He wanted to do the best he could in his studies.

They returned him to his room. They had changed room mates at the change of the semester and the room mate that he had the first half of the year came by to see him. All of the faculty, staff and the cadet regiment knew he was loosing his sight.

David said to the former room mate, "God is healing my eyes and giving me my sight back this afternoon."

With a great deal of skepticism the room mate said, "How is that?"

David said, "Let me read to you." He had been able to read slowly if he held the book about eight inches from his nose. He held up a book and read a paragraph as normal as anyone.

The other cadet said, "Don't try to fool me, you have memorized that paragraph. You can't read."

David said, "Oh yes I can." Where upon, the other cadet walked across the room and held up his hand and told David to count how many fingers he was holding up. Every time, David counted them correctly. He then held up coins and David could identify them.

He said, "Before Christmas, if you put your glasses down, I had to find them for you. You couldn't even find them yourself. Something is going on. I'm getting out of here." He left.

That evening he went to the chapel for Evening Vespers. I had visited with the chaplain on Friday. He said, "I am glad to know you. I know who your daughter and her husband are but I just have to tell you frankly, I don't believe that God does miracles today."

I said, "That's all right, I won't fuss at you, but I want you to let me believe that He does because I have seen too many of God's miracles." That was the same chaplain leading the vesper service. His also happened to be the same denomination as David Peters denomination.

David went up to him and said, "Could I have the microphone and tell about a real blessing that God has brought into my life?"

Without even questioning what it was he said, "Sure, David. Tell us about it."

David took the microphone and related the story that I have just told you, much to the consternation of the Cadet Chaplain. I want to tell you, God did restore his sight. He was able to complete West Point. He passed an Officers physical and went out to serve as one of America's fine young Academy graduates. Praise the Lord.

* * * * *

In the Spring of 1974 we were visiting our chaplains in Baumholder, Germany. It was some three hours drive from Frankfurt at night. We had a day time meeting and stayed on at the request of one of our Chaplains. We stayed in his home until it was time for his children to go to bed as we didn't get to visit with them very often. As we drove along, I said to my wife, "I sensed something is wrong in that home. I cannot tell you what it is."

She felt the same way and asked me what I thought it was. I said, "I think that chaplain's wife is going to divorce him, this summer when they get back to America." She asked why I felt that way but I had no idea. She said," That's exactly what I think."

We debated on turning the car around and returning to Bahmholder, awakening them from their sleep and saying, "What is wrong in this home?" and dealing with it. But, being human like we are, we continued on to Frankfurt, Germany.

We returned to the United States a month later. That Chaplain returned to the states shortly after that. We had mutual friends that called us and said, "Do you know that Chaplain's wife is divorcing him?" My wife and I looked at each other and realized that God had told us something and I have a little statement that goes like this. "God is not a gossip." When God tells us something, it is because He wants us to minister to that need that He has informed us about in the life of some person or family. We had failed God, when He had spoken to us in our hearts about the need in that home, and the divorce was in process.

What had happened was, the wife had completed her college degree and decided to set out on her own. The Chaplain had been so involved in good ministry, yes, even the best of ministry but she had felt neglected and not a part of it. Now she was able to independently go it on her own. Their children were still in Junior High School and that home was broken up.

When God speaks to us, we need to, at once, set about doing the thing that He has laid on our heart. We failed the Lord. May I also add here, we have seen many times when a wife finishes her college degree or nurses degree or some professional training and divorces her husband, leaves her home and leaves her children because she has been neglected and is frustrated and lonely.

Shortly after arriving in Texas, we bought a home in the suburbs of Dallas. Soon thereafter, I had an extreme severe pain that began near my back bone and came out in the left center of my chest. This had happened two or three times before and I didn't find out until some time later the cause of it.

Actually, I had a pinched nerve as the result of a bad landing on a parachute night jump at Ft. Campbell in 1958. I landed in the ditch and it threw me forward in a very poor parachute landing fall as my foot had hung in the ditch. I had pinched a nerve which resulted in a pain they thought was a heart attack. This was the third time it had happened and each time I was put in intensive care. I insisted it was not a heart attack but could not substantiate what it was. Taking precautions, the doctor put me in the cardiac intensive care unit of the VA Hospital in Dallas.

My wife would come to see me in the morning and again in the evening. It was a distance of about fifteen miles from Garland, across the city. They decided to do an angiogram to make sure my veins were open. When they did it, they proved my veins were all open and they returned me to my room and placed me flat of my back with a shot bag on the intrusion spot so the vein would close up. While I was laying there, there was no sign or symptom of a problem but the vein had been ruptured inside my stomach cavity and I was slowly bleeding to death internally with no outward symptoms. The nurse stuck her head in the door and asked how I was doing. I said, "Fine I think but I have a bit of a strange feeling." She said she would be back latter to check on me but as she turned to go I called, "Nurse, don't leave me. When you moved, I could not focus my eyes on you."

She came over and took my blood pressure and it was zero. She could not find any measurable blood pressure flowing in my body. She pushed a button and immediately there were doctors and nurses gathering around me. They were putting liquids in both ankles and both arms. Circulation began again and I was revived.

When my wife came in, here I was with four nurses and three doctors working on me. I tried to look at her but all I could see was a blurry face. They kept me there two additional days to see that my body was returning to normal and then released me to go home. It would take some two weeks for my body to re-absorb the blood in my body cavity but if they leave it alone, my blood chemistry would not be affected. If they gave me blood transfusions it may affect the chemistry. I was still a sick man but it would gradually correct it's self.

When we got home she said, "You know, the car hasn't been running quite right. Sometimes it is hard to start." When I was able I went out and raised the hood of the car. One spark plug wire had somehow moved over against the manifold and burned in two. It was a small eight cylinder engine. I thought that would cause it to miss occasionally. While I was at it, I took the distributor cap off and couldn't believe what I found. At that time there were electrical points in the distributor. The contacts on those points were both burned off. There was no way that engine should have fired a single time.

That had happened the first day I was in the hospital and here it was, a week later and the car was still running. An impossibility mechanically! The first time it had quit on her, she had laid her hands on the dash and said, "God, I am home alone. I need to go see my husband. I want this car to run until he is taken care of and out of the hospital." That car ran for a week with the points burned off and one wire to one spark plug burned completely in two.

God knows how to take care of us when we pray.

We were ministering at a Youth With A Mission Training Center in Tyler, Texas. The city had taken over an Army Air Corps field at the close of the war and it had become the municipal Airport and YWAM had the buildings on the edge of it.

While we were ministering there, I would minister to the teams in training in the day time and at night we would open it to the public.

As we were ministering one night with those who came to the altar, we had quite a line of people waiting to be prayed for. Normally, I would have people stand far enough away that the individual being prayed for would have a degree of privacy in their request for prayer.

Three young men were standing together in the prayer line. It turned out they were from a college near by. When they were at the head of the prayer line, they stepped up together. I asked what their prayer request was. They said they were all room mates. They didn't know what was going on but they had seen me pray for people who asked to be prayed for a specific item but you would pray for two or three other things in their life. They knew I was hearing from God for what I should pray so they simply wanted me to pray for them as God lead.

I prayed for the first one and when I finished, all three shook their head in agreement. I prayed specifically for three or four items. There were some pretty personal things I prayed about in the hearts and lives of all three and they all agreed. I didn't even know their names, had never seen them before or since. They said, "We have shared in our own prayer time, we have shared the evils in our lives as well as the good and God has caused you to pray for every right and every wrong that is a major part of our lives. Thanks for this time of prayer."

What had happened? I believe this, that we can pray in the Spirit, in a language we don't know and if we can get our own mind out of the circuit, we can pray in the Spirit in English and God can pray from His Spirit into our spirit, out our mouth without our mind getting involved until our ears hear that prayer as we pray out loud in our own language. There is a difficulty here in that our mind knows the words of English that we pray by the power of the Spirit of God. When we pray in the Spirit in a language we do not know our mind does not get involved and interfere. We can pray in the Spirit in our own native language if we can keep our mind out of the way, and in so doing, cause great faith to arise in the heart of the individual for whom we pray.

Gus was not a Christian, but he sometimes came to church with his wife who was. One Sunday on exiting the church, Gus said, "Pastor, you teach and preach from God's Word and from experiences of life, that God is real here and now. I have never seen God do anything that is real, that I knew was God acting in the here and now. If I could ever see God do something that is real in the life around me or in me, I might be able to have saving Christian faith."

I said, "Gus, could we meet for lunch some time this week?" He said he would like that and we picked the day. I said, "I know where your office is and I know a good restaurant near you."

He said, "Oh, no. Let's don't go there." He picked a restaurant some twenty miles away across the city. Without saying so, I knew he had picked that one because he did not want people with whom he worked, to know he was having lunch with a pastor. I didn't comment on that, I simply met him at the restaurant of his choosing.

When we got there and our meal was served, I prayed over it and I prayed that God would do something real so that Gus would know that God is alive and still working in the world today.

I had hardly finished praying when a couple entered the restaurant and walked down the aisle to be seated just past us. This was a working man whose wife had joined him for lunch. They were one of the first couples we had met when we came to Dallas and we had enjoyed their fellowship. He was hanging wall paper in a building quite near the restaurant.

Gus and I ate slowly and visited about things of the Lord and this couple ate quickly as the man needed to get back to work. As they came back down the aisle, the lady simply took my hand as it was laying there on the table, squeezed it and said "Tell your wife 'hello', we love you two." and went on. I didn't open my hand, but left it laying there on the table.

One of the things Gus and I had been talking about was financial affairs. Gus had said, "You know, if I could just hear from God, it would be so wonderful."

I told him, "Gus, sometimes God says something to us that maybe we don't want to hear." Gus asked, "Why would God do that?"

I said, "I don't know, but God is God. You know, I was saving back a little money so I could go skiing in early January." (this was early December) and I said, "Our church is buying a bus and I was praying as to whether I needed to give anything toward the bus. I had already written a check for my tithe." I had a hundred dollars laid back for my ski trip. It costs quite a bit of money to go skiing and I was hoping to save enough in about six weeks. God said, "Give that hundred dollars into the church bus." I said, "Gus, I didn't like that very well but I did what God said."

Gus looked at me. Now Gus liked money. Most of us like money but Gus really liked money. He said, "Well, I don't know if I would like that."

I said, "I didn't like it but you know God is faithful. You have probably noticed my hand has been laying here on the table for the last several minutes. As you saw, when that couple left, she squeezed my hand. Gus, she put a piece of paper in my hand. It feels like money paper to me. I want to turn it over and open it and let's see what's in my hand." I turned it over and there was a folded up $100.00 bill in my hand.

Excitedly, Gus said, "That was God putting that hundred dollars back in your hand.!"

I said, "Gus, you are exactly right. Now how many working people carry hundred dollar bills around with them?"

That woman, of a working family, had moved under the Spirit of God to show Gus that God still is active in the affairs of men and nations.

Before the week was over I received a call that there was a man coming to the Lakewood Assembly of God Church in a fine part of the city. This was a man that I had only heard of in a round about way because he had been active with the 700 Club in prior years but I had lost touch with where he was.

His name was Edwin Louis Cole, who is now head of the great men's ministry. At that time he was not so well known as he is today. When I got to the meeting, Ed was sharing with some thirty or forty ministers, the vision that God had laid on his heart about his now, wonderful, world wide men's ministry.

I had received a little more money that had come in and I had five twenty dollar bills in my wallet. We stood for the closing prayer of that meeting and God said, "Put the five twenty dollars bills you have, in an envelope and give them to Ed Cole."

Now I never put things in my Bible so I was sure I had heard God wrong. When the prayer was over I checked my Bible and sure enough, there was a new, unused envelope. I put the money in it and was not too happy when I walked forward. I hadn't even sealed it but I handed it to him and without even introducing myself, I said, "Brother Cole, God told me to give you this." and I handed it to him.

He flipped the top of the envelope open and reached in. With tears in his eyes, he said, "I really didn't have enough money to buy gas all the way back to California. Thanks."

I turned and walked away, glad that I had heard God, glad that I had met a very real and present need, but still wondering if I could go skiing.

Along in January, I said to my wife, let's go skiing. We will drive up and be very frugal with where we stay and where we eat and will make it on what we have.

We started on the trip and stopped and spent the night in west Texas with friends that had invited us. The next morning at breakfast, he said, "The Lord has laid it on my heart to have my pilot fly you to Colorado. When you are ready to come home, give us a call and I will send him back after you. I thought this was great and my face lit up I am sure.

My wife kicked me under the table and signaled me, "No, not to accept it." Our host left the room for a few minutes and she told me. "Ruth" a dear lady in our church who was a real prayer warrior and hears from God, "told me, whatever you do on this trip, don't fly in any small planes. God has said, Don't fly in a small plane!"

My wife had not felt it even necessary to share it with me as we just don't ever have the occasion to fly in a small plane.

When he came back into the room, I said, "You know Brother, I want to thank you but we are going to drive."

He was somewhat disappointed but said, "God is speaking something about transportation for you. Here is what I am going to do, take my credit card and put all of your gas on it and meals if you want to and go on your ski trip." We only used it a little bit for gasoline.

As we were going through Pueblo, Colorado we stopped to fill up the gas tank before going into the mountains. While I was putting gas in my car another car drove up on the other side of the pumps and it was a pastor I knew there in Pueblo. He wanted to know what I was doing and how long I was to be there.

He wanted us to come to the church for Wednesday night. He promised he would publicize it and have a crowd out. There are a lot of folks there who know us.

It was quite a drive back from the ski slopes but on Wednesday afternoon we drove back down out of the mountains for the evening services. We had a great service with a lot of ministry. They took up a love offering for us at the close.

We went back to the ski slopes for two more days of skiing and then drove back to Dallas on Saturday.

The bottom line is this.....We obeyed God, We got to go skiing, we were blessed in being able to minister to some hurting people, we came home with more money than we left with and we had a good time. I believe it was because we were obedient in twice giving away, what I thought, was ski money that I had been saving.

God is our source. God is greater than any need we have but we must be submissive to Him to be able to receive the blessings that our mighty God has for His children.

A lady who wanted to be prayed for to have a child was at a banquet I had spoken for at a restaurant near Ft. Hood. We had a grand evening with quite a bit of good ministry and dismissed.

My wife had gone to the back of the room visiting with old friends and Chaplain Paul Norris and I were still near the front.

Three workers were cleaning up the tables and scraping the food scraps into a plastic bucket sitting on the end of a serving cart.

The lady came up and asked if I would still pray for someone. I assured her I would. Folk often wait until everything is over to request prayer, I guess partly because it took them that long to believe it would be all right for them to ask God for a blessing.

I asked her prayer need and she said she and her husband had been married about ten years and they would like to have a baby. I assured her God answers that prayer so frequently. I have great faith, when I pray for you, you will conceive and have a baby.

I reached my hand out and lightly touched her on the forehead and said. "God, give this woman a child. You are the author and sustainer of life. Create life within her that they might have a baby in their home."

The power of the Lord came over her and she fell into the floor. As she did, she hit the bucket from the end of the cleanup cart and it flipped upside down and dumped on her face and chest. She had on a low cut blouse which was filled with mostly salad remains. Quite a bit landed on my blue suit which showed up badly.

I looked for my wife but she was in the other end of the room with her back toward me. Chaplain Norris could have helped but he was laughing so hard he had to sit down in a chair.

I reached down and wiped the food off of her face and noticed there were two peas laying on one eye lid. I looked for napkins and found some to wipe some more.

The three ladies who had been cleaning up ran from the room and soon returned with the manager who insisted he would get an ambulance. I tried to tell him it wasn't necessary, nothing was wrong with her. I finally told one of our men to take him in the other room and explain to him what had happened.

What I didn't know, was, a man had died of a heart attack there the week before and the manager didn't want to take any chances.

About then the lady sat up, put her hands in the air and said, "Oh, praise God, I have just been with Jesus! This is so wonderful." They then decided maybe she was all right.

A year later we were back in the area visiting and they said, "Wasn't that great what happened to that woman last year?" I thought it turned out all right but it was kind of upsetting at the time. They said, "Oh, hadn't you heard? She now has a three month old baby boy." God did hear and answer the desires of her heart.

✝ 30 ✝

MINISTRY IN THE AIR

I was trying to catch a plane out of O'Hare Airport in Chicago. A storm had stopped the flying, well into the night. There were no seats to set in and I had walked around for two hours to try to stay awake. Finally, one plane did take off for Europe at the next gate from where our plane was waiting to load and some seats became available. I looked around after the others had been seated, to see if there was one seat left, as I was by myself. I saw one seat at the end of a row that was unoccupied. The lady in the next seat had a baggage cart by her that was loaded down. I thought she probably had some one traveling with her, no one person would have that much baggage. I asked if the seat was free and it was.

From her coloring I thought she was probably Italian. I asked what her religious background was, expecting her to say Roman Catholic. She kind of leaned away and looked at me.

She said, "Well, I am Jewish,"

My reply was, "How should I be so blessed as to be seated here by one of God's very special Jewish people?" She asked what I meant. I said, "Oh, from my youth up, I was taught to respect the Jewish people. I'm a Christian you see and our Messiah came through the Jewish race. I am to respect Jewish people."

She said, "I never heard anyone say that. What kind of a home did you grow up in?" I told her it was a Baptist home and she said, "Oh, I work with a Baptist lady and she is always making fun of me because I am Jewish."

I said, "Mam, may I apologize for that Baptist woman whom I do not know and will probably never see. She is wrong. I want you to know I have great respect for the Jewish race that brought me my Messiah." She said she had never talked to anyone like me.

I gave her my card and told her we are a group of people that believe very much in the Holy Spirit. Referring to the Old Testament I said "In the Bible, there is much said about the anointing and about the Holy Spirit. I know that until the last days the Holy Spirit's anointing is reserved for prophets, priests and kings."

She said, "Yes, I study my Bible and my husband and I go to services regularly. I am surprised you knew that."

I told her to not be surprised, we are very much into the Spirit of God. Let me show you in the Bible, what the prophet Joel had to say. I turned to Joel the second chapter. As I turned there I asked if she believed that maybe we were getting close to the end times?

She said, "Oh, yes, we were just talking last Sabbath in our synagogue about Armageddon must surely be close at hand. All the signs and evil that is proliferating in the world and all the different things that are happening among nations. Surely Armageddon can't be very far off."

By then I had found the passage in Joel in the second chapter and I read it, which says, "In The last days, God says he will pour out his Spirit on all flesh, He will pour out His Spirit on his men servants, His maid servants. He will pour out His Spirit on the men and the women. He repeats that twice in that chapter. We believe we are so near into the end times that the Spirit of God is being poured out on all people. Not just prophets, priests and kings"

She said, "This is most interesting, tell me more." We sat there and shared the things of the Lord for about two hours until the weather cleared and they called our flight to Dallas. As we stood up I asked why she was going to Dallas. She was in the clothing business and was going to the Clothing Mart. That is why she had all of the suit cases. She asked if I was flying first class.

I said, "No Mam, I am riding near the back of the plane."

She said, "Oh, I was hoping you would be in first class and if we needed to we could change seats with someone so I could ask you more questions all the way to Dallas. You have told me things I didn't think I would ever have an answer to. I am so glad you came over and sat by me."

The world around us is hungry for that which only God can satisfy.

I was making a trip from Dallas to Charlotte, North Carolina where I was to speak at a pastors conference. I had been booked on a flight that caused me to change planes in St. Louis, Missouri. It was a foggy bad day in the wintertime. By the time we got to St. Louis it was really bad and the airport was nothing but confusion. Planes were delayed, people had missed their connections, ruining their day or maybe whole week. There was just a bad spirit in that terminal.

I had carry-on bags only and I went to the gate I would depart from. I got my back against the wall and put my bags up close to me where I wouldn't be in anyone's way. I said, "Lord, there is such a bad spirit in this airport. I don't want any of that to get off on me. I am all prayed up and ready to speak when I get to that pastors conference."

When I stopped praying the Lord said, "There is someone who will be on the plane with you going on to Charlotte that you are to minister to."

I looked around to see if I could identify who was needing ministry but I could not. There were two or three plane loads there and many of them hostile.

We boarded the plane and again, there was one empty seat on the plane, that between myself and a young lady by the window. I gave her my card, introduced myself and told her the purpose of my trip. She looked at my card and asked, "Are you a Charismatic?" I told her I was and she said, "Well, so are my parents. They are missionaries in Brazil. I don't believe any of that stuff anymore. I just finished college about two months ago. Oh, I believe there is a god somewhere, but he's not interested in us. He is way off in space. Don't give me any of this Bible stuff."

I asked, "Well, what are you doing now?"

She said, "I just came from Austin, Texas where I have a girl friend. We have been shacked up with a couple of guys for three or four days. A man I went to college with is meeting me in Charlotte and I am going to spend some time with him. I'm just flying around the country having a good time."

I thought, how calloused. Here is a daughter, whose parents have spent their hard earned, mission income, to send their daughter to a good Presbyterian college where something bad had happened to her faith.

I prayed silently, "God, give me an answer so I can reach into the heart and life of this young lady. Answer the prayers of her parents." I knew I only had about two hours to go. I asked her to tell me a bit about what was going on in her life.

She said, "Well, I'm just flying around having a good time."

"Let me ask you this. When you spend time in bed with these men, are there any strings still attached? Is it all over when it's over or is somehow a part of you and a part of them, still joined together?"

She said, "It is strange you should mention that, There really is a connection there someway, even though I intend for it to be just a one night stand."

I said, "Let me read from 1 Corinthians the 6th chapter. You have just agreed with the Word of God." I opened my Bible and read from that passage where it says, if we are joined sexually, we become a part of each other in the flesh, whether it is a love relationship or just a good time relationship or even one for hire. When I showed her that, tears came in her eyes." Let me see if we can find some other scriptures that you might agree with." I began to turn to different scriptures and in the course of that two hour flight, she got her heart and mind lined up with God. We prayed there on the plane. A couple of men across the aisle looked at me like, "What is this old man hitting on this young lady for?" She would cry awhile and then we would read more scriptures and pray again.

We ended our flight and she got off the plane. She wasn't carrying any bags and headed toward the baggage area. I was walking slower carrying my bags. I got to where I was picking up a rental car by baggage claim. There was this young lady, talking to the young man she had mentioned earlier. I remained at a distance but I saw her put her finger in his face and say something. When she finished talking to him, he turned around and left the airport hastily. I thought, "Thank God. Those parents prayers have been answered from on the Mission field in Brazil, for their daughter back home in America."

I had been visiting at the Oral Roberts University Campus. We almost always have some men and women attending there who want to become Chaplains. My wife had been on a different circuit. We call each other almost daily when we are apart but I still had several days travel before we could be back together in Dallas. I said, "Why don't we meet in Chicago this week end so we can see each other?"

Prior to boarding the plane in the Tulsa Airport, I had noticed a neat looking, well dressed lady about forty years of age, pacing the floor. As there were two or three plane loads of people in the same general area, I had no idea that she would be boarding the same plane that I was taking, but I was concerned that something was just eating on her inside to the point she could not even sit down. I said, "Lord, some way, meet the needs of this woman."

When we got on the plane, I had the aisle seat and this woman had the window seat, with the only empty seat on the plane, between us. I knew God had arranged that. I reached in my pocket and gave her my card, introducing myself as someone who worked with Chaplains.

She said, "Oh, I need to ask you some questions about Oral Roberts and his hospital. She moved into the seat next to me and said, "I'm Roman Catholic. I have just been down for my father's funeral. My father and mother had retired and moved to Florida. When he came down with cancer, he said, 'I want to be in the City of Faith Hospital, where they come by and pray for people every day. That's where I want to spend my remaining time." They had moved to Tulsa, he had died there and his desire was that he be cremated, which Catholics, in the main, do not believe in, and the ashes be spread along the sand of their beach retirement home.

I began by saying, "Let me explain to you a bit about Spirit filled people." I opened the conversation by asking, "As a Catholic, were you confirmed?"

She said, "Oh, yes, we are faithful Catholics and I was confirmed."

I asked if she remembered what the bishop said when he laid hands on her but she couldn't remember.

I told her, "I am sure you will remember when I jog your memory. A deacon, who had become an evangelist, now a Saint, had gone down to the Samaritans, whom the Jews really didn't like, and they had began to become Christians. The disciples sent their two most trusted members down to Samaria to see what was going on.

"They sent Saint Peter and Saint John and said to go see if God, indeed is accepting these Samaritans. When they got there they found out for certain that God had received them, as well as Jews.

"According to the book of Acts 8:17, they laid hands on them and said, "Receive ye the Holy Spirit." Peter and John knew that all Christians have as their birthright that they should be filled with the Spirit of God. The Samaritans were filled with the Spirit of God.

"From that time until now, all denominations who practice confirmation, use those same words. Be filled with the Holy Spirit."

She said, "Oh, yes, I understand that."

I told her, "Well, the Spirit filled people that support Oral Roberts, the University and the City of Faith Hospital, they believe very strongly in Acts 8:17. That is the kind of people they are."

She asked many questions and took notes about the things of the Lord until we landed in St. Louis. They announced we would only be there long enough to discharge a few passengers and take on a few more and we would proceed on to Chicago.

This lady said, "Can you please go out the jet-way and meet my husband? I want him to meet you. He was so upset about what my father had done that he wouldn't even attend the funeral."

I walked with the lady to the exit and said to the attendant that this lady has just lost her father and I need to take her up the jet way to her husband." I'm a minister."

As we walked out the jet-way she said, "Oh, this is so blessed, may I just hold your arm?"

Here we are, exiting that plane, into the St. Louis Airport with this nice looking lady on my arm. As we got inside the door, there was a very large handsome man glaring at me. I could see the look on his face thinking, "'Who is this with my wife?"

As we got close enough to him she said, "Oh this is a chaplain, he has answered all the questions I had about God and about being a Christian. I've made notes and I'll explain them to you when we get home but I just wanted you to meet this chaplain."

We shook hands and I hurried back to get on the plane to continue my flight to Chicago to meet my wife.

God really does care about people's needs being met.

In conclusion; I guess I should ask you: What does the future hold? What does it hold for Jim and Charlene Ammerman? What does it hold for the Full Gospel Chaplaincy? I would have to honestly answer, "I don't know." I have no idea what all God plans to do yet. I do know this, our future is in God's hands. Our lives have been in His hands. They are still there. A great and mighty God is going to do more and better in the years ahead until Jesus comes, than we have seen Him do in the past.

EPILOGUE

Years later, after I had retired, I was traveling across Germany. On this particular day it was snowing and I was going to the west side of Germany to speak that evening at Zweibrucken. I thought, with the weather worsening all the time, I may be running close on time to get there by the time the service starts. But as I passed the Landstul exit, where the largest Military Hospital is in Germany, the Lord said, "Turn off and go to the hospital." I don't know if you have ever done this or not but I have spent quite a bit of prayer time, explaining to God, the things I wasn't sure He understood. I said, "But Lord, I have a speaking engagement and with this storm I don't know if I can make it on time."

The Lord said, "Turn off for the hospital." I turned off and went back to the hospital that I had visited many times. As I did not know why I was there, I went to the Chaplain's office to see if I could decide why God had brought me. As I walked into the wing where the Chaplains' offices were located, the senior Chaplain there had just called a meeting of everyone in his section. He had been the Chaplain at My Lai, Viet Nam, so we knew each other. When he saw me he postponed the meeting until the next day and invited me into his office. When we got into the office he closed the door. Suddenly I realized why God had me there.

He said, "You know, I went through Viet Nam the same time you were there. My tour turned out all right. I wasn't wounded, I didn't lose a single Chaplain in combat. But here in this big hospital, I have taken it upon myself to be the one who visits full Colonels and General Officers. Some are brought here who are terminal with leukemia, cancer or something that is going to take their life. I have suddenly found out, I do not know how to tell them to die."

I said, "Well Brother, I know how to tell them to die." I had my Bible in my hand and I said, "May I show you what God says about it?" He said, "Please do. I need that." We sat side-by-side where we could look at the same page together from God's Word. Here was a man who was well educated, graduate of a big name seminary, a man that had been a chaplain in the military about twenty-five years, a man who had served in combat, but a man who now, in the peaceful situation of a great military hospital, suddenly realized, he did not know how to tell a person to die and meet God. Out of God's Word, we looked at those answers. Finally, I said, would you like to pray and invite Jesus into your own heart in a personal, not liturgical, but a personal relationship with the Lord Jesus Christ?

He looked at me with tears in his eyes and said, "I knew when you walked in the wing of our offices that it was something important. I have known you for years. I didn't know where you were located, but I believe God sent you by this place today."

I said, "He certainly did and I didn't want to come over here as I was in a hurry to get on down to Zweibrucken." We prayed together, and he, with joy, came into a personal relationship with the Lord Jesus Christ. I shook his hand, he hugged me, and I said I must hurry on down the autobahn.

About one year later, back in America, I was visiting in the Pentagon and asked if they knew where this particular Chaplain is now? They said, "Oh, you haven't heard? He died before his tour was up in Germany."

I had not known it, nor did he, but indeed I was telling him, how as a dying man, he could be ready to meet the Lord.